HERBS

A CONNOISSEUR'S GUIDE

HERBS

A CONNOISSEUR'S GUIDE

SUSAN FLEMING

CRESCENT BOOKS

NEW YORK/AVENEL, NEW JERSEY

Design: Hans Verkroost
Editor: Elizabeth Pichon
Production: Peter Phillips, Stewart Bowling

This 1993 edition published by Crescent Books,
distributed by Outlet Book Company, Inc.,
a Random House Company,
40 Engelhard Avenue, Avenel, New Jersey 07001

Edited and designed by the Artists House Division
of Mitchell Beazley International Ltd
Michelin House, 81 Fulham Road, London SW3 6RB

The publishers have made every effort to ensure that all
instructions given in this book are accurate and safe, but they
cannot accept liability for any injury, damage or loss to either
person or property whether direct or consequential and howsoever
arising. The author and publishers will be grateful for any
information which will assist them in keeping future editions up
to date.

Library of Congress Cataloging-in-Publication Data

Fleming, Susan, 1944-
      Herbs: a connoisseur's guide / Susan Fleming.
            p.   cm.
      Includes Index.
      ISBN 0-517-68629-5
      1. Cookery (Herbs) 2. Herbs.   I.Title.
TX819.H4F54 1990
641.6'57 - dc20   90-32881
                                                               CIP

Typeset by Hourds Typographica Limited, Stafford
Origination by La Cromolito s.n.c., Milan
Produced by Mandarin Offset
Printed and bound in Hong Kong

h g f e d c

CONTENTS

INTRODUCTION — 6–7
THE HISTORY OF HERBS — 8–11
GROWING HERBS IN THE GARDEN — 12–15
GROWING HERBS IN CONTAINERS — 16–17
PRESERVING HERBS — 18–19
HERBAL TEAS AND TISANES — 20–21
HERB VINEGARS AND OILS — 22–23
HERBS IN MEDICINE — 24–26
HERBS IN COSMETICS — 27–29
IDENTIFYING HERBS — 30

    Angelica — 31
    Balm — 32
    Basil — 33
    Bay — 34
    Borage — 35
    Chervil — 36
    Chives — 37
    Coriander — 38
    Dill — 39
    Fennel — 40
    Hamburg Parsley — 41
    Horseradish — 42
    Lovage — 43
    Marjoram — 44–45
    Mint — 46–47
    Oregano — 48
    Parsley — 49
    Rocket — 50
    Rosemary — 51
    Sage — 52
    Salad Burnett — 53
    Savory — 54
    Sweet Cicely — 55
    Sweet Woodruff — 56
    Tarragon — 57
    Thyme — 58
OTHER HERBS, LEAVES AND FLOWERS — 59–61
COOKING WITH HERBS — 62

    Herbs, Stocks, Sauces and Dressings — 63–65
    Soups and Starters — 66–75
    Fish and Shellfish — 76–81
    Poultry and Game — 82–85
    Meat — 86–91
    Eggs and Pasta — 92–93
    Vegetables and Salads — 94–105
    Desserts and Baking — 106–107
    Drinks and Preserves — 108–109
INDEX — 110–112

INTRODUCTION

Vinegars and Oils

Preserving Herbs

Botanically speaking, herbs belong to a class of plants that die down after their growing season and do not develop persistent woody tissue. This definition does not, however, take into account the many plants that are now almost universally acknowledged to be herbs – the lavender shrub and the bay tree, for instance. The term herb, therefore, has now come generally to mean any plant that is of benefit to man, one that is valued for its flavouring, medicinal, cosmetic or aromatic properties.

Herbs have an ancient and varied history, one which has developed in tandem with man, and it is interesting that only now is our technological society turning back to the knowledge enjoyed by our ancestors. All over the United States, in mainland Europe and in Britain, herbal medicine, herbal cosmetics and herbal cultivation are experiencing a renaissance. In cookery, too, herbs are once more lending their clean, fresh and subtle flavours to every sort of dish, from the simplest sprinkling of chives on a plate of buttered eggs to the most elaborate achievement of the *nouvelle cuisine*. The flavour of almost any food can be enhanced by the addition of a herb in whatever form – fresh, dried, preserved in oil or vinegar – and, when herbs are so easy to grow in most climates, there is no excuse for even the least adventurous cook not to cultivate them and use them to the benefit of every dish and every diner.

It is the essential oil of each herb that contains the aroma, the flavour and its other benefits. Many herbs are traditionally associated with particular foods, and there is often a very good reason for this: both rosemary and sage, for instance, contain oils which can help the digestion of fat, thus their culinary partnerships with lamb and pork respectively. Savory, too, contains a substance which aids the body assimilate the many vitamins and minerals of peas, beans and lentils: that it also improves their flavour and their digestibility – helping dispel the post-pulse flatulence that many suffer – is yet another bonus.

The essential oils also contain the medicinal and

Sage

Growing Herbs in the Garden

cosmetic benefits of the herbs and, even though the biochemistry of many herbal remedies may be imperfectly understood as yet, a large number have stood the test of considerable time. Some have actually been subject to pharmacological analysis: garlic, for instance, has always been known to be anti-bacterial, and the most modern research methods have now proved that garlic oil's bactericidal effect is at least twenty times greater than carbolic acid. Herbs have many other properties which are less easy to pin down scientifically, but their continual usage throughout the ages in folk medicine suggests a tried and tested effectiveness. Thus, although no-one should attempt to treat a more serious ailment with herbs without the guidance of a professional herbalist or doctor, everyone can at least try for themselves the gentle effects of herbal tisanes.

Herbs can be enjoyed in very many other ways. A large number are decorative, so look good in the garden or window box; most are aromatic, lending their scents to a room in bowls of pot-pourri, or to a cupboard or drawer when tucked into a little sachet; and they can also be used in beauty preparations. Many of the essential oils of herbs can be used to good effect when steeped in the bathwater, used as a wash for the facial skin, or when made into a final rinse for the hair.

In an age when foods, medicines and cosmetics increasingly owe much more to the laboratory test-tube than they do to nature, a knowledge of the properties and values of herbs could mean a return to simpler, more natural and more healthy living. In an age when prices are rising on every front, what could be more sensible – and economical – than growing your own flavourings, and simultaneously creating the ingredients for your own simple medicines and beauty preparations? Herbs are plants to be *used* – so why not take advantage of the cornucopia of pleasures and benefits that herbs have to offer?

THE HISTORY OF HERBS

Long before recorded history, people were using plants for food and for medicine. As they evolved, so too did the plant world, and nutritionally they would have been dependent on plants for survival – not least because three of the fatty acids essential for life are found almost exclusively in plant sources. Before they mastered weapons and tools (which enabled them to catch meat animals more easily), their diet would have consisted primarily of nuts, seeds, grains, grasses, tubers, berries, fruit and honey, supplemented by the occasional fish or small creature, all eaten raw before the discovery of fire.

Although it would have been a case of trial and error at first – perhaps even of life and death – people would gradually have become familiar with the properties of plants: those which nourished them and those which affected the way they felt. Animals, after all, have always instinctively sought out healing plants when they were unwell. Once this knowledge was established, it would have become part of their lore or heritage. A mystique would have grown up, echoed in much of the folklore of the succeeding centuries: when

Animals naturally value the healing powers of herbs.

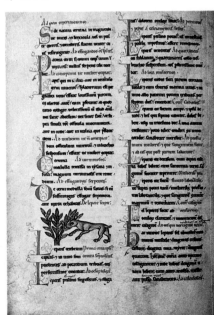

was most propitious to plant herbs; to which god a herb should be dedicated or offered; and how best to pick herbs. (The Druids, very much later, believed that the latter was best done, naked, at the time of the full moon.) The Upper Palaeolithic cave paintings at Lascaux in France date from as early as 18,000BC and, amidst the ochre and sepia oxen, deer and horses, are pictures of medicinal and food plants. It is thought that the creatures stone-age people hunted were depicted so frequently because they believed they would thereby remain plentiful; this may well have applied to their depiction of plants as well. And indeed, when plants were so basic and influential a part of life, it is easy to understand why many came to be looked upon as possessing magic or supernatural powers.

When, about 15,000 years ago, the ice sheets retreated northwards and the climate improved, people were able to form settlements: no longer were they obliged to follow the migratory herds for food and move to where plant foods were in seasonal abundance. Now it was possible for them to actually harness the provisions of nature, and the earliest agriculture is thought to have begun between 10,000 and 5,000BC in a belt stretching from northern Greece to Iran and from Jordan to the Crimea. It was here that the wild ancestors of goats and sheep thrived and where the primitive forms of wheat and barley grew wild. This is also, interestingly, the approximate area from which a majority of our present-day herbs originate.

The Great Civilizations

With the dawn of the great civilizations – from roughly 4,000 years BC – we have the first records, many of which show how herbs were used and valued as both food and medicine. The Sumerians knew medicine, had a rudimentary knowledge of anatomy, and understood the medicinal properties of such plants as thyme: in about 2,200BC tablets were inscribed with a list of a thousand plants. In Babylon and Assyria, too, a herbal medicine flourished. But it was perhaps in Ancient Egypt that the use of herbs and plants was most widespread: papyri from as early as 2,800BC record herbs being used for food, medicines, cosmetics,

perfumes, dyes and disinfectants. They also left herbs like rosemary in the tombs of their Pharaohs and high officials to ensure their safe and comfortable journey to the hereafter. Coriander seeds have been found in tombs as well, and are mentioned in the Ebers papyrus along with a great number of herbal and aromatic mixtures designed to treat a variety of illnesses. The Egyptians had a great knowledge of the culinary value of herbs and spices too, adding them to their dishes of millet and barley to make them easier to digest, as well as much tastier! They used coriander seeds in wine to increase its intoxicating power, as well as mint, sage, marjoram (sacred to the god Osiris), and parsley; and garlic's healthy and bactericidal properties were recorded in an inscription on the Pyramid of Cheops – each slave was given a clove daily to keep him good health during the pyramid's construction. The preservative properties of herbs were used also in the Egyptian art of embalming: thyme oil was a constituent of embalming fluids.

The sea-faring Phoenicians who traded all around the Mediterranean were probably responsible for the spread of herbs and much of the herbal lore at this time. It is known that the Hebrews, for instance, already used herbs as food; and the Old Testament records the bitter herbs to be eaten during the Passover. Hyssop was one of them, and it was also the herb used to mark the doorways of the children of Israel with blood. And that herbs were a major part of diet elsewhere is perhaps exemplified by "Tollund man", a stone-age man put to death by strangulation. Found in a peat bog in Denmark in 1950, he had lain perfectly preserved by the tannic acid in the bog for over 2,000 years. Even the contents of his stomach were identifiable – barley, linseed, fat-hen seeds and sorrel.

It was in Ancient Greece, however, that the herbal tradition continued. The most famous Greek doctor was Hippocrates, the fifth-century BC "father of medicine", whose writings and practical observations were to have an influence upon medical science until the eighteenth century. Up until that time, ignorant of the physical causes of disease, most primitive peoples had believed illness to be caused by evil spirits or to be a punishment for sin. Hippocrates, however, founded a rational school of medicine and

Hippocrates, the "father of medicine".

A contemporary of his was Pliny the Elder, a Roman, whose *Natural History* contained over 30 volumes, and was a compilation of many Greek and Roman sources.

For the Romans, too, revered herbs, and after their conquests they absorbed much of the knowledge of the Greeks, Egyptians, and Hebrews. Like the Greeks, they would use herbs in worship, in ceremonial, strewing them on floors, burning them as incense, and lavishly, along with spices in their cookery – for the Romans apparently liked strong flavours. They were keen gardeners and, in the time of the Empire, had hothouses with glass panes. Martial refers to hothouse-grown fruit and grapes as well as plants for decorating the house and the heads of dinner guests – the Romans believed crowns of flowers or leaves such as parsley, roses or violets would protect against drunkenness!

It was principally the Romans who were responsible for the spread of herbs throughout Europe. The legions would carry their herbs and seeds with them and settlers would plant their gardens with the herbs without which they thought they could not survive their exile, both in terms of medicine and food flavouring. Many hardy herbs like fennel would thus become naturalized, growing as escapes along the coastlines and near to houses and towns; it is even said that many herbs found growing frequently on roadsides in Britain mark the routes taken by the legions. Some 200 herb varieties are believed to have been introduced to Britain by the Romans, among them lemon balm, borage, coriander, hyssop, lavender, mint, parsley, rosemary and thyme. During the 400 or so years of Roman occupation the use of these introduced herbs, both in cooking and medicine, would undoubtedly have become familiar to the native British.

The Middle Ages

After the fall of Rome, during the period that is generally called the Dark Ages, civilization may have declined in Britain and elsewhere in Europe, but herbal lore continued and was handed down amongst the people from generation to generation. Herbs were useful in preserving meat – and improving its flavour – during the winter months; and mint has been giving its savour to lamb and mutton since the days of the Romans, as has sage to pork and goose. Herbs were used for medicinal purposes, and each village would have had its wise woman who would have a wide knowledge of plant remedies and superstitions (which would lead, inevitably, to the later witch burnings, with the clash between the Church and such "pagan" beliefs).

Herbs were also used in beauty preparations and for perfume. At this time and for many years after, personal and domestic hygiene was not considered a priority, so herbs were used to counteract

divorced diagnosis from religious belief or mere speculation, believing that disease was caused by imbalances in the body. He also averred that diagnosis of disease had to be based on reason and detailed observation. He wrote many books on the subject of diet, health and hygiene, including about 400 herbal remedies or herbal simples.

Later, Dioscorides, a first-century AD Greek naturalist and physician to the Roman army, wrote a book which, like the work of Hippocrates, was to have an enormous influence on healers and the use of plant drugs for centuries thereafter. (In fact, it is interesting that the recently dedicated American National Herb Garden, in Washington D.C., has several garden sections, and one of these is devoted to the medicinal herbs listed by Dioscorides.) As he travelled around the Mediterranean with the Roman armies, he collected hundreds of plant, mineral and animal specimens. He then described them – first-hand observations rather than hearsay or superstition – in *De Materia Medica*. One of his discoveries was that the juices from the bark and leaves of the white willow eased aches related to colds and fevers. Today such ills are treated by aspirin tablets which are totally synthetic, but their natural ancestor was the active compound found in the very same willow trees that Dioscorides studied.

unpleasant smells. Until the late eighteenth century, the stone, wood or earth floors of houses in Britain and in Europe would be strewn with rushes interspersed with antiseptic and insect-repellant herbs like rue, hyssop and savory; sweet-scented herbs would also be added, like thyme, lavender and mint. The floors of churches would be covered with special herbs, usually marjoram and rosemary, and herbs were strewn on the floors of the law courts to disguise the smells which must have been rampant in such public and crowded places – and to prevent the judges being infected by the prisoners. The antiseptic powers of herbs were thought to be so great that people would carry "tussie-mussies", small posies or nosegays of mixed herbs, to ward off the plague. And during the Black Death of 1348 and further attacks of the decimating bubonic plague in the fourteenth century in Europe, as well as during the Great Plague of London in 1665–1666, doctors and many others would wear nosebags or masks containing spices and herbs, or would wear pomanders around their necks, to protect against contagion.

In Britain the cultivation of herbs and a herb medicinal tradition was continued formally by the monks in monasteries founded after the establishment of the Christian church. Early Saxon herbals display a wide knowledge of many herbal cures – for monks would have been the "conventional" healers of the day, practising medicine from their infirmaries. As well as tending the herbs in their "physick" gardens, they would have been copying out manuscripts from the ancient writers. The

The title page of a 1588 edition of Hippocrates.

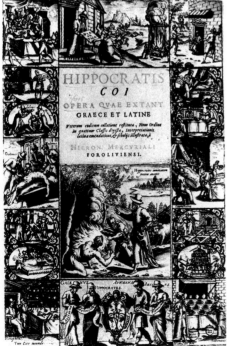

tenth-century *Leech Book of Bald,* the first to be written in the vernacular instead of Latin, was influenced by many European herbals, dating back to *De Materia Medica.*

Medical and botanical researches continued in other cultures. The Arabs were to the fore in the rest of the world, and many manuscripts show illustrations of physicians supervising work on medicinal plant gardens. They also carried on the cause of "rational" medicine, translating the works of many classical scholars. Avicenna, for instance, a tenth-century Persian physician, discovered how to distil the essential oils of herbs and flowers while studying the properties of plants. In India, too, doctors were developing a formal knowledge of plant drugs and their effects. A drug used to tranquillize in the treatment of modern mental illness was refined in the 1940s in America from a plant called rauwolfia: this same plant had already been in use in India for the same purpose for over 1,000 years.

The Age of the Great Herbals
The medicinal and culinary uses of herbs reached their climax in Europe during the sixteenth and seventeenth centuries. Herbals were being published in Italy and Germany in the late fifteenth century, and the science of botany was growing fast. The discovery of America in 1492 and the explorations of this time were to lead to a huge kindling of interest in new plants; and the invention of printing was to introduce properly the age of the great herbals. The dissolution of the monasteries in the 1530s meant that more people took to growing medicinal herbs themselves now that the infirmaries of the monks no longer existed: medicinal, cosmetic and culinary lore was passed down as before from parent to child; herb women and root gatherers from the country plied their fresh wares in towns; and physicians relied to a great extent on their herb gardens.

Printing made herbal information very much more widely available, and influential at this time were the works of Dodoens, a Belgian physician, and Mathias de l'Obel, a Frenchman who spent much of his life in England and later became botanist to James I of England (VI of Scotland). William Turner – known as "the father of English botany" – travelled widely studying plants before writing his books, *The Names of Herbes* (1548) and his *New Herball,* published in several instalments after 1551. But the most famous herbal of the period must be that of John Gerard. He had a physic garden at Holborn in London and superintended for 20 years the gardens of Lord Burleigh in the Strand, and at Theobalds in Hertfordshire. His *The Herball or Generall Historie of Plantes* was published in 1597, and there has been some dispute as to his source, primarily, it would appear, an unpublished translation of

Illustrations from Gerard's Herbal *of 1636.*

Dodoens. However, the book is packed full of lore, botanical information and culinary suggestions, and it is still almost constantly in print some 390 years later. In it, for probably the first time, are described many of the new plants which had been introduced following the discovery of the New World – among them the Jerusalem artichoke ("But in my judgement, which way soever they be drest and eaten, they are a meat more fit for swine, than men"), the potato, tomato (he called them "Apples of Love"), and tobacco, to which he ascribed many virtues of which present-day doctors would scarcely approve.

While Europe was enjoying the new-found fruits of the great explorations of the period, the New World itself was enjoying a herbal revolution. An American herbal had been written in 1569 by a Spanish doctor called Nicholas Monardes (his name is recorded in the botanical name of bergamot, *monarda didyma*). In it he wrote of many of the herbs found by the early settlers, who in their turn had taken with them many European herbs without which they could not survive. This massive interchange and relocation of plants – for the discovery of America had doubled the range of food plants known in Europe – can only be paralleled in significance by the introduction of herbs to other countries by the Romans as they advanced northwards

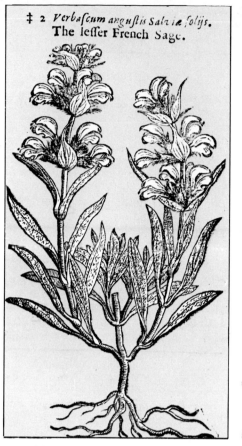

‡ 2 *Verbafcum anguftis Salviæ folijs.*
The leſſer French Sage.

† 3 *Phlomos Lychnites Syriaca.*
Syrian Sage-leaued Mullein.

some 1,500 years earlier.

To ease the rigours of wilderness life, the colonists would have to rely on herbs for fresh greens, teas, tonics, dyes, insect repellants, deodorants and medicines, and they would also have carried with them some of the European herbals, from which they could concoct herbal potions. Native plants, too, whose secrets were learned from the Indians, began to be used – chief among them bergamot – and many of these were sent back to the newly founded botanical gardens of Europe – the Jardin des Plantes in Paris, the Italian gardens in Florence and Padua, and the British gardens, the first at Oxford, founded in 1621 (the year after the Pilgrim Fathers landed in Massachusetts), and later, those at Chelsea and Kew.

Further herbals were published in England throughout the century, among them that of John Parkinson, apothecary to James I and botanist to Charles I. Nicholas Culpeper's *The English Physician,* published first in 1652, although full of good information on all manner of herbs and their properties, almost single-handedly ruined the reputation of herbs and the scientific advances that had been made in herbal and general medicine. For much sensible advice is interlaced with astrology – all the herbs come under the influence of a particular planet – and the philosophy of the book harks back in no small way to the ideas of Paracelsus who had propounded a doctrine of signatures some

1000 years earlier. This "signature" aberration decreed that as plants were put on earth by God for man's use, those plants were all marked with some kind of stamp or signature which would make their medical purpose clear and obvious; so plants with heart-shaped leaves were to be used for heart complaints, for instance. Although Culpeper drew forth the scorn and dismay of his contemporaries (he was equally as scornful of them in turn), his entertaining herbal is continually in print.

The Modern Age

Although the use of herbs declined in Britain during the eighteenth and nineteenth centuries, a herbal tradition survived in less industrialized countries in Europe and in America. In the latter it was kept alive primarily by the Shaker sect who grew and marketed herbs on a large scale, culminating in the foundation of a famous garden in New York in 1820.

However, as the Industrial Revolution in Britain brought people from the countryside to the towns, so herbal cultivation and traditions disappeared until, from the mid-nineteenth century onwards, the only herbs in common culinary usage were the famous four – the "parsley, sage, rosemary and thyme" of the folksong "Scarborough Fair". As commercial food flavourings were manufactured and sold, culinary herb gardens were no longer cultivated. In fact

most people no longer could grow their own food, so industry had to take over, and, in the interests of profit, and what has come to be known as "shelf-life", foods were laced with the chemical additives against which there has currently been such an uproar. To most alternative or holistic medical practitioners, the diet of western society today bears the main responsibility for many of our twentieth- century illnesses; through eating "unnatural" foods we have fallen victim to "unnatural" illnesses, many of which are unknown or rare in less industrialized countries. It is ironic that the enormous medical advances of the last century or so have marched hand in hand with the diseases induced by poor diet.

And, as medical and pharmaceutical discoveries advanced – many of these based on the isolation of active plant principles and the laboratory reproduction of them – so, too, herbal medicine virtually disappeared. Patent medicines rapidly took the place of herbal remedies, and a strong and healthy tradition was lost.

It is only now, perhaps, in the latter half of the twentieth century, when people are becoming more aware of health and are dissatisfied with the side-effects of strong modern drugs, that herbs and other plants are once again being recognized as having a definite place in everyday life. In a culinary sense, herbs have been part of a dramatic revival on both sides of the Atlantic; they have brought back a fresh taste to foods that have for too long been processed, and artificially preserved, coloured and flavoured. Cosmetically, the preponderance of plant extracts in preparations such as shampoos, creams and lotions, shows the direction in which the public and thus the commercial interests are going.

Medicinally, herbs are also enjoying a come-back, with formerly "alternative" therapies like homeopathy, aromatherapy and herbalism itself increasing in popularity. Pharmacologists in the large drug companies too are turning once again to the plant sources. The World Health Organisation has begun to show an interest in herbal medicine, and is working in tandem with many countries where the prime mode of curing is based upon plants. This combination of modern science and ancient knowledge must hold enormous potential for the future.

Botanical and herb gardens are flourishing in America and in Europe, and plant sources are being researched and analysed for old, forgotten or new properties – medicinal, cosmetic, agricultural and industrial. The potential of the active principles of plants is enormous, and probably less than half of those that could benefit man have been identified so far. Herbs will obviously continue, therefore, to play a major part in our history for some time to come.

GROWING HERBS IN THE GARDEN

The herb garden at Butser Ancient Farm in Hampshire in which some of the beds are devoted to plants used before the Roman occupation, and others to species introduced thereafter.

herbs. Some can withstand quite cold temperatures, but most dislike cold wind, and so a hedge or wall or even some sturdy shrubs or bushes should ideally be near the herb garden to act as a wind break.

Given all these considerations, the actual size of the site for the projected herb garden isn't really important. If space is at a premium – in a small town garden, for instance – herbs can be grown in containers of various sorts (see page 16); they can be slotted into the herbaceous border – angelica, lovage and some fennels make a good backdrop, and chives, parsley, lady's mantle, marigolds and marjoram would make interesting edging plants as they are low growing. Some herbs can be grown in a rockery – lemon thyme, chives, marjoram, rosemary and lavender – and many herbs could actually form small hedges – rosemary, hyssop, rue, sage and lavender.

But if there is a specific larger area which can be given over to a proper herb garden, then you can have great fun designing it. There are many good gardening books and books on the history of gardens which detail the intricacies of the formal herb and knot gardens of the past, with their patterns of leaves and flowers, small herb hedges, paths and divisions. Look also at the gardens in the grounds of historic houses which will show you their beauty and potential, and give you many varied ideas. There are now a large number of commercial herb gardens and nurseries which will also inspire you.

Preparing the Herb Garden

Once the site has been chosen, the soil should be prepared. Although herbs grow happily in most sorts of soil, a slightly alkaline soil is preferred. It should not be too heavy or rich, and it should be well drained. No soil is so poor that it cannot be improved in some way or another: even exhausted, sour and thin city soil can be dug and enriched by bought humus, peat, manure, or by well rotted compost. Dig over the soil – preferably in autumn to allow time for the winter frosts to break it up further – and fork in one or more of the above.

Compost is one of the most economical ways of enriching the soil in your garden in general. Build a heap in a secluded part of the garden or buy a proprietory compost bin (they are also very easy to make). Use layers of garden refuse: lawn trimmings, fallen leaves, plucked weeds etc, all but the woody stems which would not easily break down. Use organic kitchen waste as well – vegetable and fruit trimmings (never again feel guilty about disposing of those outer cabbage or

A nyone with any sort of garden space at all should allow room for some herbs. They are easy to grow, do so mostly on a small scale, and are undemanding plants. They also have many benefits, not least their culinary, medicinal and cosmetic uses: they can be most decorative, many serve as good ground cover, some have startlingly beautiful flowers, and the majority are highly aromatic.

Planning a Herb Garden

As herbs are plants to be *used*, perhaps the first consideration is the proximity of the projected herb garden site to the kitchen. Somewhere near the back door, normally the nearest to the kitchen, is ideal, as you don't want to have to plough across acres of wet lawn or fight your way through prickly

foliage every time you want a sprig of parsley.

The second consideration is position and siting of the herb garden as regards sunlight. Most herbs come from fairly dry and sunny areas – thyme, marjoram, oregano, rosemary and sage, for instance, all hail from the Mediterranean – and many need as much as seven hours of sunshine per day in the summer. A number of herbs prefer to be grown in dappled sunlight or partial shade – generally speaking, this means the juicier green herbs such as chives, mint, chervil and parsley – so they require at least four hours of sun per day. Very few herbs need complete shade, but some, like sweet woodruff, would wither and die if exposed to full sunlight.

A third consideration is shelter for the

Grow herbs in herbaceous borders, in a sunny position near the back door, or in a more formal arrangement, enclosed by a low hedge.

sprout leaves), tea leaves and egg shells.

Many herbs themselves are useful in compost as their properties help the heap's conversion into humus: the nearby roots and leaves of elders apparently encourage this; and yarrow, chamomile, comfrey, dandelions and nettles also speed up and enrich this conversion if included in the heap (nettles contain iron and nitrogen; dandelions copper; and comfrey is almost a herbal fertilizer in itself as its leaves contain potash, nitrogen and phosphorus). Last year's dried herbs can be flung on the compost heap, and many herbal infusions can be used as a compost "accelerator" (proprietory varieties are also available). A well composed and drained compost heap should be ready for use within about eight weeks in the summer, about double that time in the winter.

Dig the soil over once again in the spring, digging in yet more humus, firm it down and the bed will be ready for planting in a couple of weeks.

Choosing Herbs for the Herb Garden

The ultimate choice depends on the gardener and on what he or she wishes to grow, although the nature of the site and the garden will dictate terms to an extent as well. A certain amount of knowledge (a lot can be gleaned from simple research) is vital at first. You want to know the heights of plants: those which grow tallest, for instance, will obviously need to be planted at the back of a border herb plot, or in the centre of a more formal circular or square herb garden. You want to know the nature of the plants concerned, and whether they will spread or cross-fertilize: mints, horseradish and tarragon all spread by creeping root systems so these should be "contained" in some way, and the plants should certainly be given generous space all of their own. Different varieties of mints will cross-fertilize as will dill and fennel, so they should be kept apart. You want to know also the pattern of growths of herbs so that you can keep the herb garden looking good at all times, without bare gaps where perennials have died down in the winter. Some evergreens will be useful, and do try to have a good variety of mixed annuals and perennials.

It is leaf shape, colour and texture that provide interest in the herb garden so this is another consideration. Some herbs have pale or silver leaves (lavender, mint, rue, sage, thyme); some are variegated (mints, pelargoniums, sages, thyme, lemon balm); some are dark green (bay, fennel, tansy); and some are gold (feverfew, varieties of marjoram and thyme). Although most herb flowers are insignificant, a few are larger, so you should try to include a few of those: bergamot has extrovert red flowers; borage and hyssop are blue; lavender is a cool mauve; and some chamomiles, as well as marigolds and nasturtiums, have cheerful orange and yellow flowers.

And don't forget that herbs can be grown as an aromatic lawn or between paving stones, so that they exude fragrance every time you step on them – chamomile, pennyroyal mint and thyme.

Growing Herbs

Some herbs – the annuals and those which self-seed but which for the purposes of cultivation are treated as annuals – are freshly grown from seed each spring. Buy seeds from a reputable seed company; the packets usually have good information and

Heel cuttings *Strip a sturdy young side-shoot from parent stem.*

Trim the tail, dip in hormone powder and plant.

Root division *Carefully lift parent plant and shake off soil.*

Cut off a piece with a developed bud and replant.

instructions on them.

Water first then sow the seeds thinly in the enriched soil when the weather is warm and all frost damage is quite past. Cover them with a little more soil, and mark the spot where you have sown them. Most annuals will germinate within about a fortnight – although parsley, for instance, is notoriously slow. Most perennial seeds can take up to 4 weeks to germinate, so do take care to mark their position or you could mistake them for weeds and pluck or hoe them out!

When the seedlings reach the four-leaf stage – at a height of about 2in/5cm – they can be thinned out and replanted to the required distance apart. You could of course plant seeds first of all in seed compost in a seed box inside or in a greenhouse; cover with a sheet of glass and newspaper. This will speed up germination, and when the seedlings are the required size and have been transplanted into larger pots, you can harden them off before planting outside in their permanent positions.

Many herbs can be bought as plants from nurseries – a more expensive way of establishing a herb garden, perhaps, but often not so painful for the less green-fingered! Indeed some herb seeds are so rarely available that the only alternative is to buy them as plants. Some, too, are so slow or difficult to germinate, that bought or donated plants will be more useful – and encouraging – in a new herb garden. These include sage, rosemary, lavender, parsley, marjoram, woodruff, lemon balm, and lemon verbena. Dig a hole in the prepared and chosen site, and water it well. Decant the plant from its pot, gently spread out the coiled-round roots, and insert the root/soil ball into the hole. Firm soil around the stems and water well. Garlic and horseradish require different treatment. Plant garlic cloves from a bulb in well prepared soil, pointed end up, and water well. Cut horseradish thongs into lengths, and plant thick ends uppermost. Water well.

Maintenance of a herb garden is fairly basic. The herbs need to be well watered, particularly during dry weather, and they need to be kept scrupulously clear of choking weeds. They are subject to few pests or diseases but do look at them every now and again to check. (If mints show signs of rust on their leaves pull out the plants and burn them.) Pick leaves as required and cut off flower heads to encourage foliage growth, unless you wish to allow some to remain for seed. At the end of the growing season, cut back shrubby herbs such as rosemary; cut down fleshy stemmed plants and preserve the leaves for winter. Label any perennial plants such as comfrey which will die down in the winter – or you may forget where they are. Many plants in fact can be dug up and put into pots to over-winter indoors (as long as they are not too large): parsley, bay, rosemary, thyme, marjoram, tarragon, salad burnet, lemon verbena and summer savory all benefit from being brought indoors. Put them in roomy pots, and allow a few days outside before bringing them in, to a cool room at first.

Propagation of Herbs

Other ways of initiating or supplementing a herb garden are by cuttings, layering, root division or by gathering seeds from established plants. Many indeed are self-seeding (among these are borage, dill, angelica, chamomile, lemon balm, salad burnet, chervil, coriander, comfrey, hyssop, fennel and sweet cicely), but self-seeded seedlings can be a nuisance from the point of view of clearing, weeding and fertilizing the soil, and they can take over the herb garden if you're not careful. (See pages 18–19 for some ideas of how to harvest seeds, whether for cultivation or for cooking.)

Take soft or nodal cuttings in spring from shrubby herbs such as lavender, rosemary, sage and hyssop. Remove the top 3–4in/7.5–10cm of a vigorous shoot of new growth (not one with buds) and pull away the bottom leaves, leaving about three to four sets of leaves. Pinch out the growing tip, dip the base in hormone rooting powder and press into rooting compost around the edge of a pot. Have three or four plants in one pot. Water well, place in a cold frame or greenhouse – or bring indoors, the whole pot encased in a spacious plastic bag, held on with an elastic band. The cuttings should root in about four to six weeks, after which they should be moved on to individual pots with more nutritious soil before hardening off and planting out.

Take hardwood or heeled cuttings from herbs such as thyme in May or June, and bay, sage, rosemary, hyssop or lemon verbena in late summer. Strip away a young side shoot from the parent stem so that a heel – a tail sliver of bark and wood – also comes away at its base. Trim the tail on the heel and any nearby leaves. Dip the heel in rooting powder and plant immediately as for soft cuttings. These may take longer to root.

Many herbs whose stems form roots if kept in contact with soil can be layered in spring. Press a long portion of root runner or stem into the surface of the soil – or into a pot of compost if the stem is long enough to reach – and hold it down with a loop of wire or an old-fashioned wooden clothes peg. If the stem is thick, make a little cut in the underside and dust some rooting powder into it. When roots have formed, cut the umbilical cord between child and parent. Herbs which can be propagated in this way are thyme, winter savory, the mints, sage, rosemary, marjoram and lemon balm.

Root division is carried out in autumn or early spring when the herbs are dormant and there is no danger of frost. Done regularly, this will quickly produce many new plants and will also help prolong the healthy life of the parent. It is suitable for many herbs, among them the mints, tarragon, tansy, bergamot, sorrel, lemon balm, sweet cicely, comfrey, oregano, and woodruff and for the tiny bulb clumps of chives. Dig up the parent plant, shake off the soil, and divide the roots carefully. If roots are very tangled or the creeping stem is too tough, cut cleanly into them with a sharp knife. Replant the divisions as quickly as possible and water well until they become established.

GROWING
HERBS
IN
CONTAINERS

As herbs can be grown in even the smallest patch in the garden, so most of them will flourish happily in pots or other containers, to be kept either indoors or outdoors.

Herb Containers Outdoors

Those with a small city garden may not have even the smallest plot available in which to plant herbs, and container growing is often the only answer. In patios or courtyards, old clay sinks or large wooden tubs or troughs may be used for growing herbs; on flat roofs or balconies where weight might be a problem, modern plastic versions, if not so visually pleasing, would be a sensible alternative. Herbs can also be grown outside in hanging baskets, in pots wired to a board attached to a wall, and in window boxes. Half tubs or barrels can be bought, old chimney stacks can occasionally be found, and large strawberry pots and barrels could also be pressed into service.

Many of the strictures which apply to herbs grown in the actual garden apply also to container-grown herbs outside. They must have sun, partial sun or shade, according to species, and they prefer to be sheltered from cold winds. One advantage of container growing, however, is that, if the containers are neither too large nor too heavy, they can themselves be moved so that the plant can have more or less sunshine as it needs.

The most important consideration when growing in containers is that of the growing medium. A shop-bought ordinary potting

Left, a spacious potting shed at the Royal Horticultural Society's gardens at Wisley. Right, a small outdoor trough holding essential culinary herbs.

compost is better than garden soil; and if you're worried about the ultimate weight of the container on a balcony, say – for a container full of wet compost is *very* heavy – lighter varieties of compost are available.

Any container should be well washed before filling, and it must have some sort of drainage. An old sink will have a drainage hole: cover this with broken crocks (use pieces of broken clay flower pots) so that water can drain out without it getting clogged up with compost. Wooden tubs or troughs should have plenty of drainage holes and these too need to be covered with pebbles or broken crocks to a depth of about 2in/5cm (or, again, if worried about weight, use chunks or shapes of polystyrene). To avoid rot, and to encourage the circulation of air, wooden containers should stand on bricks ideally. Do remember, too, that once these larger containers are filled with the growing medium, they will almost certainly be too heavy to move, so fill them only when they are placed in the correct position.

Hanging baskets can easily be bought, and they look very pretty when planted with herbs that trail. These need to be lined first with a thick layer of sphagnum moss – sometimes even a thin sheet of plastic – so that no soil will fall through. Pots that are hung on wire loops from a board on a wall –

or simply from supports in a wall – need pebbles for drainage in the normal way; and window boxes should have drainage crocks and should stand in a drip tray to protect the fabric of the window ledge.

Fill containers with growing medium so that there is a space of about 2in/5cm at the top; this allows for a little more soil to be added when seeding or planting, and also helps avoid any overflow of soil when watering. Sow seed or plant when the growing medium has been well soaked. Remember to water regularly, particularly in hot weather, as water evaporates more quickly from containers; if the soil is dry on top and to a depth of about 1in/2.5cm, the plant needs watering. Hanging baskets require special attention. A fine spray of water will help all herbs, but do so in the evening when the sun is down. Weed meticulously as herbs growing in a confined space need all the goodness they can get out of their own "patch" and shouldn't have to compete with anything else. As container-grown herbs need a richer soil than garden grown, they should be given a liquid feed every 2 weeks or so during the growing season, between May and September.

Remember to protect certain container-grown herbs in the winter. Bay trees, rosemary and verbena bushes should be pulled under cover if possible, or the base of the stem or trunk should be kept warm by layers of sacking or straw. Bring inside pots of the more tender herbs such as pelargoniums, basil, rosemary, marjoram, lemon verbena and summer savory. Every March or April, remove about 3in/7.5cm of soil from the tops of tubs or troughs containing perennials such as bay, thyme or sage, and replace with fresh compost.

Herb Containers Indoors

Many herbs will grow very satisfactorily indoors although, lacking space in which to grow and with a more limited light, they will be smaller in general than herbs grown outdoors. They can be grown in a greenhouse, sun room, glass-covered balcony, or on sunny windowsills.

They should be grown from seed and planted as above, potted in clean pots, with a good growing medium – a richer one than that used for outside container-grown herbs – and drainage crocks at the bottom. Their greatest need is for light, so have them in a south-facing room if possible where they can get sunlight for at least a major proportion of the day. However, too much sun at the hottest time of the day can scorch tender leaves through glass; and you should try to turn them every now and again.

Fresh air is another major requirement of indoor herbs, especially if they are growing in the stuffy, steamy atmosphere of a kitchen. When it is warm, they will enjoy sitting beside an open window – so long as there will be no sudden draughts of cold air, as fatal to a a tender herb as to the most exotic house plant. If possible, herbs can be taken outside for a while in warm weather, perhaps even into a warm and gentle summer shower; they will relish the change.

Temperature is another consideration. You should not attempt to grow them on a windowsill above a radiator, for instance, as this will be far too hot and drying; the ideal is warmth during the day – of about 60°F/16°C – and a cooler temperature at night. Humidity is important as well, so in a centrally heated environment, a saucer or bowl of cold water near to the plants will ensure a moist atmosphere.

The watering and feeding of indoor herbs need particular attention. If over-watered, herbs will soon die; they will die too if regularly left *without* water. The pot should sit in a saucer or drip tray, on top of a layer of pebbles; these will lift the pot fractionally so that the soil is not in constant contact with water and the herbs won't get

waterlogged. Many indoor herbs will need an occasional fine mist spraying of water which not only refreshes them directly, but can also free their leaves of household dust. Try to use water that has been sitting in jug or watering can for a while; cold water from the tap can often be far *too* cold. Feed indoor herbs about every 10 days.

But even despite regular feeding, plants in small pots soon deplete the soil, and indeed grow too big for their pots. Try to re-pot herbs every year in fresh soil, and plant others in larger pots when roots start to show through the drainage holes in the foot of the pots. Propagate indoor herbs in the same way as herbs grown in the garden. Harvest leaves, too, in the same way, depending on species, pinching out growing tips and flowers to encourage bushier growth.

Pests and diseases are few – and indeed many herbs are reputed to keep insects away. But indoor pots of herbs like basil are sometimes prone to greenfly. If you can, pluck these off gently with your finger, or, if they're too many, dip the whole plant gently, upside down, into a bowl of warm, slightly soapy water.

Herbs for Container Growing

It is perhaps easier to define those which *cannot* be grown in containers, as the majority of herbs will happily flourish in them, indoors or outdoors. In general, the larger plants – many of the *umbelliferae* family, which includes dill and fennel – and those which have large tap roots are the ones which are best grown in the garden proper. Only if outside containers are really large and deep, could you perhaps cultivate angelica, dill, fennel and horseradish; the first three can achieve an enormous height, and horseradish's invasive roots need a good depth of soil. They would all be much better in the garden. Elder and wild roses are unsuitable for container growing, as are borage and comfrey, both of which have long roots. Garlic is best grown in the garden as is coriander, the initial smell of which might be rather unpleasant if grown in a pot in an enclosed space. Lovage would never reach its full height potential if container grown, and woodruff likes to creep over shady ground, not round a container.

Almost everything else can be grown, with a greater or lesser degree of success, in some

sort of container. Many can be grown side by side in the same container, but one rule to remember is that they should all share the same sun and watering needs. You could have a large pot either indoors or out holding the essentials for a bouquet garni, bay, parsley and thyme; the bay will obviously grow larger than the other two, so ensure that it does not overshadow them. You could have a window box or a couple of pots with fresh herbs for winter consisting of salad burnet, thyme, sage, winter savory, and marjoram (and don't forget about the greens still available from Hamburg parsley and dandelions in the garden). A summer selection could be parsley, basil, chervil, chives and summer savory. You could have a windowbox full of herbs to scent a room: among the aromatics are lavender and the pelargoniums. A few pots of herbs suitable for tisanes could include peppermint, chamomile, hyssop and lady's mantle.

Another rule involves the invasivity of root systems which is particularly pertinent to container growing: the mints should perhaps be grown in containers on their own; lemon balm, tarragon and yarrow should be grown in individual pots as they can take over and choke any neighbours.

A sunny windowsill shows how decorative mixed pots of herbs can be, here complemented by dried bunches hanging up.

PRESERVING HERBS

There are several ways in which the fresh flavour of herbs can be preserved – by drying, freezing, salting, preserving in oil or vinegar, by transferring flavour to a sugar syrup (or indeed to a sugar) and by candying or crystallizing. Drying and salting were once the principal methods available, but since the advent of freezing, many more herbs can be kept fresh and colourful, ready to lend their bouquet to cooking at all times of the year.

The important thing to remember is that fresh herbs are usually better than preserved for most purposes – culinary, cosmetic or medicinal – and thus it is only really worth while preserving the herbs which are not available during certain parts of the year. Woody perennials like rosemary and thyme, for instance, are evergreen, so can be plucked fresh at any time, and parsley can be grown indoors in pots the whole year through.

Harvesting Herbs
When harvesting herbs for preserving, there are a few important rules to follow. The best possible time for herb leaves to be harvested is at a very precise moment in their life cycle – after the flower buds have formed, but before those buds actually burst into flower. At this time, the essential oils and other properties of the herbs are at their fullest, the foliage is most abundant, and the flavour is at its most intense. After this, the plant's energies will go into flowering and producing seed, which means in some herbs woody stems, a paucity of leaves, and a weaker flavour. All herbs produce buds at different times, so you should watch them carefully, and the approximate harvesting times below might help. If you want to harvest a herb's flowers, do so just before they are fully open. If you want to harvest a herb's seeds, gather these when the seed heads turn brown.

April/May (late spring)	Harvest chervil leaves and woodruff.
June/July (early summer)	Harvest angelica leaves and stems, coriander, lemon balm, lovage, parsley, rue and tarragon leaves; rose petals.
July (midsummer)	Harvest basil, feverfew, eyebright, hyssop, marjoram, mint, rosemary, sage, tansy and thyme leaves; borage leaves and flowers, chamomile, elder, lime and marigold flowers.
July/August (late summer)	Harvest lemon verbena leaves; lavender flowers; sweet cicely seeds.
September/October (early autumn)	Harvest summer savory leaves; rose hips; and the seeds of celery, coriander, dill, fennel, lovage.
October/November (late autumn)	Harvest the roots of angelica, Hamburg parsley, horseradish and valerian.

Harvest herbs on a dry morning. Wait just long enough for the dew to have evaporated from the herbs, but not so long that the sun has reached its hottest. Gather whole stems or leaves as appropriate in smallish bundles: speed is of the essence when preserving, as any delay reduces the properties of the herbs, and you don't want to pick more than you can cope with in a short space of time. Gather them carefully too, as you don't wish to bruise them; this also releases the volatile oils which hold the flavour. If harvesting from annual herbs, the whole plant can be dug up afterwards and put on the compost heap; the same can apply to biennials unless you want to save a few to set seed. With perennial herbs, take care not to weaken the plant by taking too many leaves; ideally a third at least of its leaves should be left.

Drying
This is the preserving method most commonly used although, paradoxically, it can be one of the least successful with many herbs. It is only practical in the case of a few plants whose essential oils can survive the drying process, but a large number of others are dried, of course, for different uses such as in tisanes and pot-pourri.

The herbs that dry best for culinary use are lovage, marjoram, mint, sage and savory;

The autumn "fruits" of a successful kitchen garden – among them the herbs lavender and rosemary.

these all retain completely their flavour and colour if dried properly. Other herbs that dry comparatively well are celery leaves, marigold petals, oregano (its flavour is perhaps best when its dried), lemon balm, borage flowers, bergamot flowers and leaves, sorrel, nasturtium leaves and woodruff. Bay, rosemary and thyme all dry well but as they're evergreen, they could be picked fresh throughout the winter. Salad burnet too dries well, but as it stays green in the winter, there is no real necessity to do this.

Among the herbs which do not dry at all well are many annuals like basil and borage, and some members of the *umbelliferae* family – chervil, coriander, dill, fennel and parsley. With most of the latter, the seeds can be dried and used for flavouring when leaves are not available (although all can be successfully preserved in other ways). Tarragon and chives also dry poorly.

Bring the herbs in from the garden, and pick them over carefully for any damaged or diseased leaves. Depending on species, separate into leaves or sprigs, or tie together in bunches. Wash only if absolutely necessary. There are three basic ways in which herbs may be dried, and the essentials in each case are shade (bright light draws the colour from the herbs), and air (warm, dry air must circulate to drive out the moisture).

An old-fashioned method is to hang bunches up in a dry, airy, shady room; if you're doing a lot, then bunches could be hung from a washing line strung across that room. Dust could be a problem, in which case paper (not plastic) bags tied over the bunches will protect them – and can also catch seeds from drying seed heads.

Another, more reliable, way is to place leaves and sprigs in a single layer on a muslin or cheesecloth covered rack, cover loosely with more muslin, and leave in the same dry, airy and shady room. Depending on temperature and herb, drying can take from two to seven days, but it can be accelerated by using an airing cupboard.

The third method is more successful with the fleshier herbs like sage, mint and lovage, and for delicate flowers. Put the herbs carefully on trays and put them in the oven at the lowest possible setting; hold the door slightly open with a wooden spoon handle. They should be dried in about an hour. Herbs could also be dried successfully in a microwave oven.

Herbs are dried thoroughly when they are brittle, breaking when touched rather than bending. Crumble leaves very slightly and place in clean, dry and small dark glass or earthenware jars: if clear glass is used, the herbs will have to be stored away from light. Leave some sprigs of rosemary and thyme whole as they'll be easier to pluck out of a casserole dish after they've completed their flavouring work; and for the same reason try to leave a stalk on bay leaves. Label each jar carefully with the name of the herb and the date dried, and use within 6 months. And never waste old dried herbs – throw them on the compost heap or the soil around pot plants.

When using dried herbs in cooking, always spoon them out of the jar into the dish rather than shaking them out of the jar over the dish; steam could be absorbed by the herbs left in the jar and they would become damp. And lastly, never forget that the flavour of herbs concentrates when they are dried, so use only one-third dried of what you would use fresh.

Other Uses of Dried Herbs

Many herbs are dried for use in teas and tisanes (see page 20), and for perfuming the home in pot-pourris, herb sachets, or pillows. The latter capture the scents of summer all year round, look good, are easy to prepare, and make very good gifts for friends. Mix together a selection of the pot-pourri herbs mentioned throughout the book – flowers, petals and leaves – and add spices like ground cloves, cinnamon or allspice, fixatives like orris root powder, or a proprietory "pot-pourri maker".

Herb sachets can scent drawers, cupboards or suitcases while you're travelling – and can also keep moths and other insects away. Make little flat cushions from a lining material and stuff with selected herbs – lavender, woodruff and lemon verbena are good – and then make a cushion cover from a pretty cotton material that can be removed for laundering. Herb pillows are simply a larger version, and can be used instead of a pillow or under a conventional pillow to induce restful sleep. Lavender, lemon verbena and peppermint are particularly sweet smelling; angelica, bergamot, lemon balm, marjoram, rosemary, thyme and woodruff can all aid sleep.

Freezing

This is perhaps the most successful way of preserving herbs, with the colour being retained as well as the full flavour. The only disadvantage is that thawed herb sprigs are limp and cannot, therefore, be used for garnishing. Freezing is most suited to the delicate herbs which cannot be dried – basil, chives, chervil, dill, fennel, parsley and tarragon. Sorrel, coriander and salad burnet also freeze. Store all for up to 6 months only.

Wash, drain and dry herbs thoroughly. Place them in freezer bags – chives in bunches, basil, briefly blanched, in twelve-leaf portions, parsley in heads, and chervil, tarragon and dill in small sprigs – and place bags in tightly sealed and labelled plastic boxes (to prevent other foods absorbing the herb flavour). Basil leaves could also be painted carefully with olive oil and then frozen in one layer between sheets of wax/greaseproof paper.

Herbs could be finely chopped before freezing. Parsley can be stored in handy-sized screws of aluminium foil, but one of the best ways is to pack chopped herbs into individual ice-cube trays which are then filled up with water and frozen. The herb cubes can simply be melted in a dish during cooking or, if the water content of the cube is not required – in a butter sauce, say – the cube can be thawed in a sieve and only the chopped leaves used. This ice-cube idea can also garnish summer drinks: freeze individual borage flowers or aromatic leaves like lemon balm in ice cubes.

Chopped herbs can be frozen ready for use in herb butters (see page 65). Try any of the above, or use a *fines herbes* mixture. Elderflowers, geranium leaves and sweet cicely can lend their aromas to a thin sugar syrup which can be frozen for use as a base for making sorbets.

Salt Preserving

Basil and coriander can be preserved in salt and oil as described on page 22; both the leaves and the oil can be used in cooking thereafter. Other herbs like parsley and chervil can be preserved in salt alone: layer the chopped herb up with coarse salt in a dark jar and cover lightly. Keep for several months, well sealed and covered to exclude all light. Remember to take the salt content into consideration when cooking.

HERBAL TEAS AND TISANES

Before the explorations of the Elizabethan age, and the opening up of new trade routes (which allowed for the introduction of a wealth of spices), herbs, flowers and plants in general were the only source in Britain of food seasonings and medicinal and cosmetic preparations. They were also the only source of warming and refreshing drinks – the "infusions", "cordials" and "waters" prevalent before the introduction, in about the mid seventeenth century, of the new foreign herb, tea (the leaf of a camellia tree grown in China). Soon all the old leaf or herbal concoctions became known as "tea" as well: even the medicinal spa waters of Bath were once called "limestone tea".

The new drink quickly became popular, but only amongst the wealthier patrons of the coffee houses – in 1660 Pepys was trying his first cup. The price would have been beyond the means of all but the richest to begin with, as it was in such short supply and so highly taxed: all this contributed to the (now very collectable) tea caddies with locks to deter theft, and a lucrative trade by the servants of the rich in selling used and re-dried tea leaves! And it is undeniable that the British taxing of Chinese tea imports to America – which caused the Boston Tea Party of 1773 – directly contributed to the continuing unpopularity of tea-drinking in America (Americans drink twenty times more coffee than they do tea, while the British drink five times as much tea as coffee); it is also highly probable that this led indirectly to the continued thriving of an American *herbal* tea tradition, a tradition that became all but lost in Britain once Chinese and Indian tea imports became plentiful and the price decreased.

Why Drink Herbal Teas?
Despite their undoubted popularity, Indian and Chinese teas, it is now known, are not particularly beneficial to health. The leaves contain tannin and caffeine and, perhaps surprisingly, they are one of the major sources of fluoride. Tannin in too large doses – a well "stewed" cup of tea – can actually tan the stomach lining: anyone who drinks tea without milk will know of the brown stains left on the inside of cups. Caffeine, a stimulant, can lead to an "addiction", and can be the cause of many complaints ranging from dyspepsia and migraines to heart palpitations. Fluoride, although generally considered beneficial (to the teeth), is in fact a poison, and a compulsive tea drinker could be ingesting the mineral in excess.

To return to the tradition of herbal teas, therefore, would seem to be a good alternative. Herb teas – or tisanes as they are called in France, and a name which is becoming more current in English – are flavourful, refreshing, can be made in a multitude of varieties, and they can positively contribute to health. They do not contain tannin, caffeine or fluoride, but have properties which can soothe, refresh, relax and invigorate; many are so mild in their therapeutic properties that they can be given to children. Altogether they make a valuable addition to the diet if taken on a regular basis, but it must also be stressed that moderation is important: an over-enthusiastic consumption can be ill advised, and can occasionally have some disagreeable side-effects.

With such a choice of herbs now available in herbalists' and health-food stores, whether loose in packets, or as tea-bags, herb teas can be drunk at breakfast time – an invigorating one would be best – and for afternoon tea; herb tea-bags can be used in an office situation just as easily as traditional tea-bags, and they would be much more sensible than endless stressful cups of coffee. Many teas – lemon balm, for instance – are thought to possess brain-stimulating properties; and a digestive and calming tea would be the ideal way in which to round off an evening meal. Indeed in France and in other countries on the Continent, where the herbal tradition has never faltered, it is quite common for customers of restaurants and visitors in private homes to ask for a particular tisane of choice.

Changing to Herbal Teas
Many think that making herb teas is complicated and time-consuming, but exactly the same principles are involved as in making ordinary tea: heating the pot, popping in the herb, and pouring over boiling water. In fact many herbs require only a minimal infusion for their fragrance to be released into the water. Many claim that the flavour of a number of herb teas

leaves something to be desired – and indeed a few can be bitter – but it is a matter of gradually re-educating the palate, or simply adding a little honey to sweeten to taste. You can experiment with herbal teas, mixing two or more varieties of herbs together, to get the desired flavour; you could also add other ingredients such as a little orange peel (delicious in basil tea), or a lemon slice or piece of lemon peel. To ease the transition, you could make your own "blend": add a little fresh or dried herb of choice to a traditional tea infusion. This was an early economy measure – continued during British wartime rationing – with the precious Indian tea being eeked out with additions such as blackberry tip leaves (these gave a stronger colour). In fact many teas are already blends of some sort or another: mint tea in Morocco is made from gunpowder (green) tea and mixed with fresh and dry mint leaves; and jasmine tea, the tea commonly served in Chinese restaurants, is a mixture of green or black China tea leaves and jasmine flowers. You could mix up in your tea caddy a combination of your favourite tea along with a selected dried or fresh herb; if left for a while, the flavours will meld.

You could also emulate the flavours of favourite teas with varying quantities and combinations of herbs. Once you get to know your favourites, you will be able to make a fairly informed guess as to how they will inter-react. In *Food in England*, Dorothy Hartley suggests a herbal tea mixture of hawthorn leaves for bulk, with sage, lemon balm, woodruff and blackcurrant leaves for flavour (blackcurrant leaves, however, contain tannin). If sage were to be in a greater proportion, she suggested the tea would taste rather like a fragrant Ceylon tea; if lemon balm predominated, the tea would resemble China tea; and if the hay-like fragrance of woodruff were to the fore, the tea would approach the smokey and tangy flavour of a Darjeeling.

Particularly Good Herbal Teas
Most of these teas are discussed elsewhere, along with their basic and medicinal properties, but those opposite are the most widely available, the ones with the most pleasant tastes, or teas which are rather more unusual.

Bergamot

Bergamot oil is added to black tea leaves to make the distinctive Earl Grey tea: this oil is obtained from an orange tree, not from the herb, but the flavours are not too dissimilar. Bergamot herb tea, made from the flowers or leaves, has a slightly bitter taste; leaves can be added to China or Indian tea as well as to wine drinks and lemonade. It can be made by infusion or, to achieve a rich red colour from the flowers, by decoction (simmer for about 5 minutes). It is soporific, and is therefore ideal for a nightcap.

Chamomile

The flowers only – fresh or dried – are used for a tea which has a slightly bitter, but pleasant and very delicate flavour. It is good when taken after meals, soothing and aiding digestion.

Ginseng

The root of ginseng has been used medicinally in China for about 5,000 years, and has enjoyed a vogue in the West rather more recently. It is believed to be a cure-all, a universal panacea, as well as an aphrodisiac, and many are convinced of its efficacy on all points. A tisane tastes faintly of licorice, and ginseng is also one of the many herbal ingredients of a strong spicy Japanese tea called *mu*.

Lemon Balm

One of the most useful of herbal teas, as it relieves fatigue and tension, aids the brain and memory, and is reputed to prolong life! The leaves, fresh or dried, are deliciously lemon flavoured, and can quite happily be steeped for longer than other herbs.

Lemon Verbena

The leaves of lemon verbena, fresh or dried, make a fragrant and delicious tea. It can be drunk hot or iced, can be blended with mint, and is sedative and digestive.

Lime

The flowers make a herb tea which, like chamomile or mint, is drunk as much for its delicious flavour as it is for its medicinal properties – relaxing, mildly sedative and digestive. The tea can be drunk hot, or cold and mixed with lemonade. The leaves also make a good tea.

Mint

All of the mints can make tea, but peppermint possesses the most medicinal properties, as well as the best flavour, with a menthol coolness. Spearmint is sharper and more aromatic. The leaves can be used fresh or dried, and a mixture of the two makes for a wonderfully refreshing drink.

Raspberry Leaf

The dried or fresh leaves make a light tisane which tastes faintly of the fruit. It is good for female disorders, and is particularly renowned for its simulating effect, before and during childbirth. The leaves should be steeped for about 15 minutes.

Rose Hip

The dried pods and pips (they are available from herbalists and health-food stores) should be very finely crushed and steeped for about 7 minutes to make an astringent tea. This is ideal for adults and children alike as it contains such a high proportion of vitamin C. It will probably need sweetening with honey, and the C can be intensified by the addition of a slice of lemon. It's also good with some ground hibiscus added, deep red with a citrus flavour. Rose-hip tea is diuretic, and can help those who are slimming.

Yarrow

The fresh leaves and flowers are rich in vitamins and minerals, and a tisane is good for the stomach. A dried leaf or flower tea can also be prepared. It is slightly bitter, but has stimulating properties.

HERB VINEGARS AND OILS

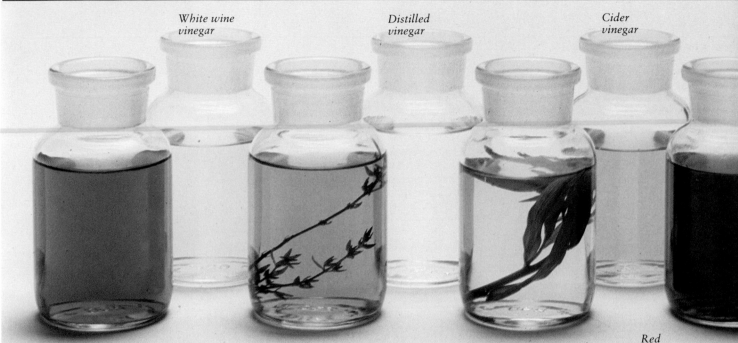

White wine vinegar *Distilled vinegar* *Cider vinegar*

Malt vinegar *Thyme vinegar* *Tarragon vinegar* *Red wine vinegar*

Vinegars and oils are essential ingredients in everyday cookery, and each varying vinegar or oil lends its own distinctive flavour to a dish. But when a herb is steeped in an oil or vinegar base, the flavour of the herb – as well as its beneficial essential oils – permeates the base and transforms it into something very much more subtle and special. These herb-flavoured oils and vinegars have a prime place in cooking, naturally, and a larder stocked with different varieties gives the cook endless possibilities for unusual variations on familiar dishes. They can also, however, be used cosmetically and medicinally. And, purely from an aesthetic point of view, a jar or bottle of a golden oil or burnished vinegar with a few delicate herb sprigs suspended in it, looks most attractive and enticing.

Herb Oils
Oils can be extracted from nuts, seeds, fruits, vegetables, flowers and beans, but the ones to use for herb oils are those with the blandest, least pronounced flavours – although an exception to this rule is olive. The best to use are sunflower, safflower and corn: they are high in polyunsaturates so are more healthy as well. Other possibilities are grapeseed and peanut oils. A mild olive oil

will benefit enormously from the inclusion of herbs; a richer virgin olive oil needs little to enhance it, but it too could be used thus.

Herb oils are extremely simple to make, and they look and smell as delicious as they taste. Indeed some herbs are best preserved in oil – basil and coriander, for instance. Try if possible to start making herb oils in summer, as sunlight is necessary for the aromatic oils to filter into the base oil.

Wash the herbs well and pat them dry. Using a good 2 tablespoons crushed herbs per 1¼ cups/300 ml oil, put the herbs into an appropriately sized bottle, and cover with the oil. If you like you can use slightly less oil, adding about 1 tablespoon of white vinegar (or vodka) which gives a tang. You could also simply fill a jar with crushed bunches of herbs and cover them with oil. Seal tightly with a plastic cap or a cork (never metal), then put the bottle or jar into a position where it will receive a good proportion of sunlight (in sunny climes they are left to mature in the open air). Leave for at least 10 days before using, longer if necessary or preferred. Agitate the bottle or jar a couple of times a day, every time you pass perhaps. To make the oil stronger you could strain it of the first lot of herbs after about 2 weeks, and repeat the process with

freshly cut and bruised herbs. The oil is ready when it tastes and smells strongly of the herb – a little on the back of your hand should readily proclaim its major influence.

If there is not enough sunshine, you can "cook" the oil in a bain-marie. Place the jar or bottle, tightly sealed, in the water of a water bath, and heat gently, keeping below boiling point. Do this for a couple of hours each day for a week. The process could be repeated with fresh herbs, but the oil should be ready after about 7–10 days of this treatment.

As a final and decorative touch, add a sprig of the fresh or dried herb to the strained oil. Label carefully, with the ingredients and date made, and use lavishly.

Herb Oils in Cookery
Flavoured herb oils can be used in almost everything, but they are most associated with salad dressings and marinades. Always select an oil to complement the dish. A basil oil would be delicious in the dressing for a tomato salad; it can also be drizzled over the top of a simple pizza before baking. A fennel oil would be ideal to use in a sauce or marinade for fish, or in a mayonnaise to accompany cold fish. A tarragon oil would blend magnificently into a mayonnaise for

Spirit vinegar with lemon

Mint vinegar

chicken salad, and a rosemary oil could be brushed over lamb steaks or chops before grilling (and, if barbecuing, don't forget the sprigs in amongst the embers). Fry calves' liver in a sage oil, marinate mushrooms in a thyme oil dressing, and use a savory oil dressing for a bean salad. Potatoes fried in a herb oil have a magnificent flavour: try rosemary or thyme. Olives steeped in marjoram or oregano oil taste as if they'd never left the Mediterranean. Other herbs which flavour oils superbly are bay and coriander.

Herb Oils in Medicine and Cosmetics

Certain polyunsaturated oils – the ones mentioned above – are good for health anyway in that they replace others which are high in saturated fats; and a certain intake of oil is necessary to enable the body to absorb fat-soluble vitamins like A and E. When herbs are added to these oils, along with their reputed medicinal properties, the value of the oil in cooking is amplified.

Herb oils could also be used as massage oils to relieve pain: particularly associated with these powers are bay, marjoram, rosemary and thyme. A small quantity of a flavoured oil for this purpose could be quickly made by heating about a cupful of a

bland oil with a handful of fresh or dried herb: balm and lavender in particular leave the skin smelling wonderful. Use warm.

Herb oils can be used for hair conditioners – rosemary and sage are obvious choices – and also to perfume home-made creams and moisturizers. Perfumed oils can be used in the bathwater – perhaps along with a sprig of the appropriate herb – for a fragrant, skin-softening and relaxing bath.

Herb Vinegars

Herb vinegars have a wonderful flavour, and add tang to any salad or marinade – or indeed to a casserole or sauce as a finishing touch. Once much more widely used – they were a favourite in Mrs Beeton's day – flavoured vinegars have gradually come back into fashion, with raspberry vinegars featuring in many dishes in top restaurants, and tarragon vinegar available commercially. However, it is best – and fun – to make them at home, and they can also be used medicinally and cosmetically.

The best vinegars to use are the cider or wine vinegars which will not obliterate the delicate flavours of the herbs. One exception is horseradish vinegar which could be made with malt. Use red or white wine vinegar: red for garlic, say; white for tarragon, basil or salad burnet; and cider for mint. But, as with anything, you can happily experiment.

Pick the herbs just before they flower, wash and dry well, then put the leaves and soft stalks, slightly bruised, into a large jar. Use a good 3 tablespoons herbs to 5 cups/1 litre vinegar. Cover with vinegar, seal tightly (with cork or plastic, never metal which causes an adverse chemical reaction with vinegar), and leave in a dark place (so that the herb colour is retained) for at least 10 days, and up to 8 weeks! Shake or agitate the bottle or jar at least once every day, as with a herb oil. You can strain and repeat the process with fresh herbs if you like, as for herb oil again, and really the vinegar is ready when it is pungent with the herb, or when you feel it's strong enough for your purposes. Strain it into bottles through a funnel and add a sprig of the fresh herb to make it look good. Label carefully – adding the ingredients, the date, and perhaps the time spent steeping as a reference for the future – and use lavishly.

Herb Vinegars in Cookery

As with oils, use herb vinegars in dishes which will be complemented by the herb. A mint vinegar would be wonderfully

refreshing in salad dressings and ideal for a fresh mint sauce. Horseradish vinegar (which will only take about a week to reach its full, and very powerful, strength) would be best used in dressings to accompany a beef salad – and the horseradish left over after straining would be used in a sauce for roast beef. Make a mustard with a herb vinegar for additional tang, use lemon thyme in a mayonnaise, and dill in a dressing for cucumbers. A salad burnet vinegar would impart a wonderful cucumber flavour, especially appreciated by the many who suffer digestive problems with real cucumbers. Tarragon vinegar – perhaps the best known of all – is the one to use in a classic Béarnaise sauce. A garlic vinegar is useful as well: add 2oz/50g crushed cloves to 2½ cups/600 ml white wine vinegar and leave for 2 weeks.

Other herbs which make successful vinegars are basil, bay, borage, chervil, lemon balm, fennel, marjoram, savory, rosemary, thyme and, perhaps surprisingly, chamomile, elderflowers, lavender, nasturtiums, rose petals and violets. Herb mixtures are possible too: try savory, marjoram, chives and tarragon; or basil, bay, mint, rosemary and tarragon.

Herb seed vinegars can also be made: bruise seeds (coriander, fennel, dill etc) in a pestle and mortar, using about 3 tablespoons seeds to 5 cups/1 litre vinegar. Warm the vinegar and pour over the seeds in a large jar. Cover tightly and place in a warm dark place for about 2 weeks, shaking occasionally. Strain when ready.

Herb Vinegars in Medicine and Cosmetics

The skin has an acid mantle, and vinegar can be very helpful in restoring its proper balance. Quick herb vinegar remedies can be made by heating a herb in vinegar then leaving to steep and cool for a couple of hours. To cure an itchy skin, for instance, a cup of an appropriate herb vinegar added to bathwater can work wonders (lavender would be deliciously fragrant). Similarly, vinegars are useful in tonics for the facial skin; make up a mixed herb vinegar (lavender, tarragon and rose petals, perhaps), and keep a bottle beside the bath or on the dressing table, diluted eight parts water to one part vinegar.

Hair, too, benefits from herb vinegars. A red wine and rosemary vinegar (diluted as above) is good for dark hair; a chamomile and white wine vinegar rinse for fair hair.

HERBS IN MEDICINE

The use of plants to cure disease is as old as the human race, perhaps even older, as animals have always sought out particular herbs or grasses when they are unwell – present-day domestic dogs and cats still eat grass when they feel off-colour. Man has been dependent on the plant world for existence in a nutritional sense throughout much of his history; it was inevitable, therefore, that a knowledge of herbal medicine would evolve. At first, it must have been a discovery rather by trial and error – for many plants *are* poisonous – but records from Ancient Chinese and Egyptian sources show a sophisticated and considerable knowledge of the medicinal properties of plants. This culminated in the great herbals and pharmacoppias of the Middle Ages and after.

Although herbal remedies have become less valued since then – their usage being finally overshadowed by the advent of the synthetic drug industry – they survived in folk medicine in various cultures throughout the world, and herbal medicine or herbalism is now becoming popular once more in the West. To some extent this is because many are disenchanted with the strong chemicals and side-effects of many modern drugs, but it is also because many pharmacologists have begun to re-evaluate the properties of plants which have long been thought to be healing. Indeed many modern drugs are based on plant compounds: morphine for pain control (from opium poppy heads), digitalis for the heart and other cardiac ills (from the purple foxglove), and a cancer-fighting substance used in the treatment of leukaemia (from the leaves of the Madagascar periwinkle). Feverfew and the evening primrose are but two of the plants which have come to recent prominence and are under proper scientific evaluation: the first because of its undoubted remedial effect in the treatment of migraines; the acid contained in the oil of the second are proving useful in such varied areas as eczema, heart disease, pre-menstrual tension and hyperactivity in children.

For safety, if you are unsure you have made the right plant identification, it is perhaps best to use only herbs that have been bought from a herbalist – although most of the common herbs are easily recognizable. If you are in doubt about whether a herbal remedy should be tried for an ailment – or if you have a bad reaction – seek the advice of a herbalist. The potential power of herbal treatments should never be underestimated. Some herbs, just as some drugs, can have side-effects, can have addictive properties, and should always be taken in a sensible way. Moderation is the keyword, even with the most gentle of herbal remedies.

How to Make Medicinal Preparations

There are many ways of making and applying herbal preparations. Infusions, decoctions and teas are principally for internal use; compresses, poultices and oils for external use – but sometimes the methods of usage are interchangeable (decoctions and infusions, for instance, can be used for external beauty treatments). Whichever method chosen, it is the essential oil that is the valued part of the herb, so every drop must be extracted. And do remember that any home-made remedy, precisely because it does not contain any suspect preservatives, should be used up quickly as it will not last.

Infusions

These are the simplest herbal remedies, and they can be made with dried or fresh herbs, from the leaves, flowers, petals, or soft stems, depending on variety. Bruise fresh herbs slightly first, and then pour boiling water over them – 1oz/25g fresh herb to 2½ cups/600ml boiling water. If using dried herbs, use ½oz/15g herb to 2½ cups/600ml boiling water. Cover tightly, and allow to infuse for about 5–10 minutes before straining. Use hot, warm or cold, and within a couple of hours while fresh; if it is to be drunk, sweeten to taste with a little honey.

Decoctions

These work on virtually the same principle, but can be used to extract the utmost goodness from harder stems, roots and seeds, as well as dried or fresh herb leaves or flowers. Using the same ratios of herb to water, soak the herb or pounded stem, root or seeds in cold water for at least 10 minutes before bringing to the boil in an enamel (not metal) saucepan. Cover and simmer for about 5 minutes, then leave to steep for at least another 10 minutes. Cool, strain and use.

Compresses

These are used externally, and hot or cold depending on the effect required. Soak pieces of lint in a very strong herbal decoction and hold over the affected area (or bandage in place). When a cold compress warms through contact with the skin, replace with

An eighteenth-century pharmacist dispensing his multifarious wares.

another cold one; when a hot compress becomes cold, replace that as well, and repeat the process.

Poultices
These are applied externally, usually hot. The herb is bruised and pulped, mixed with a little hot water, and applied directly to the affected area; alternatively the herb can be encased in muslin or cheesecloth and soaked before application. Dried herbs could be mixed with a paste of flour and water and then applied.

Ointments
These are made in a similar way to herbal beauty creams, but petroleum jelly is used as the base instead of a cold cream. To every ¼lb/125g jelly, add 1oz/25g crushed herb, and simmer together for 15–20 minutes.

Oils
Many herb oils are as good for embrocation and massage oils as they are for beautifying and culinary purposes. See page 22.

Teas
These are a basic herbal medicine, and one of the most simple and pleasurable ways of taking herbs for health. See page 20.

Inhalation
Some herbs can be inhaled to relieve the stuffiness of a head cold or to give a general benefit. Steep a herb in boiling water as for an infusion, and use as for a facial "sauna" (see opposite). Inhale deeply while the face is over the water; or use the chosen herb in the bathwater, when its effects will, obviously, be milder.

Specific Herbs for Use in Medicinal Treatments
Most of these are used in teas or infusions; some are made into decoctions and poultices, etc, for external use.

Refreshing and Tonic
Borage, dandelion, elderberry, nettle, parsley, rose hip, rosemary, sage, salad burnet, savory, violet flowers, woodruff, yarrow.

Relaxing and Sleep-Inducing
Angelica, basil, bergamot, chamomile, dill, lemon balm, lime flowers, sage, thyme, valerian, verbena, woodruff.

Antiseptic, Antibiotic, Disinfectant
Basil, chamomile, chives, coriander, garlic, horseradish, lovage, marjoram, mint, nasturtium, oregano, rosemary, sage, thyme.

Cleansing
These are the herbs which are principally associated with internal cleansing and blood purifying. Many are diuretic in action.

Retain the steamy heat using a towel.

Borage, chamomile, chervil, chives, dandelion, elderflowers, hyssop, lovage, nettle, parsley, rose hip, salad burnet, sorrel, woodruff.

Headaches and Migraines
Angelica, basil, chamomile, feverfew, mint, lavender flowers, lemon balm, lime flowers, rosemary, sage, thyme, violet flowers, woodruff.

Colds and Sore Throats
Basil, bergamot, chamomile, comfrey, eyebright, fennel, garlic, horseradish, lime flowers, lemon balm, lovage, nasturtium, pennyroyal, peppermint, sage. Particularly good for a feverish cold are elderflowers and yarrow; for a head cold and stuffiness, angelica, basil, chamomile (the latter two as inhalations), eyebright, fennel, lime and sage.

Fevers
Basil, bay, borage, chervil, elderflowers, lemon balm, lime flowers, marigold flowers, sage, woodruff.

Catarrh
Borage, coltsfoot, comfrey, horseradish, hyssop. Once used as a snuff to clear nasal congestion were coltsfoot, basil and marjoram.

Chest Troubles and Coughs
Angelica, basil, bay, coltsfoot, comfrey (root), garlic, sage, thyme and yarrow. Particularly associated with hayfever and asthma are eyebright, hyssop, lavender, marjoram, oregano, sage and thyme.

Digestion
Angelica, basil, chamomile, chervil, chives, coriander, dandelion, dill, fennel, garlic, horseradish, hyssop, lime flowers, lovage, marjoram, parsley, peppermint, rosemary, sage, savory, sweet cicely (leaves and roots), tarragon, thyme, verbena.

Flatulence
Angelica, basil, dill, lovage, parsley, peppermint, rosemary, savory, sweet cicely, thyme and yarrow.

Constipation
Basil, dandelion, feverfew, parsley, yarrow.

Nausea
Basil, chamomile, lemon balm and mint.

Slimming
Fennel, parsley, rose hips and sweet cicely.

To Benefit Specific Organs
Borage, garlic and lemon balm are believed to be good for the heart; chamomile, dandelion, dill, horseradish and mint for the liver; and chives and yarrow for the kidneys. Sorrel and salad burnet benefit both liver and kidneys; woodruff, the gall bladder and liver; rose hips, the gall bladder and kidneys; and tarragon the heart and liver.

Menstrual and Female Disorders
Basil, lady's mantle, rue, tarragon and yarrow.

Pain-Killing
Lemon balm, mint and rocket.

For Stings, Itches and Rashes
The simplest and most familiar herbal cure is the crushed dock leaf on a nettle sting, but there are a few others: chamomile (good for nappy rash), feverfew, hyssop, a poultice of horseradish, parsley, savory or thyme.

For the Teeth and Mouth
Good mouthwashes are made from infusions or decoctions of chamomile flowers, comfrey, lemon balm, marjoram, rosemary, sage, sorrel, thyme and violet flowers. The oils of marjoram and peppermint are good for toothache, and an old remedy for this was to chew the leaves of yarrow. Sage is thought to whiten the teeth.

Wounds and Cuts
Poultices of comfrey, marigold petals, and yarrow; ointments of comfrey and lady's mantle.

Rheumatic Pains
Chervil, dandelion, nettle, parsley, sage.

Bruises, Aches and Pains
Chervil (warmed leaves as a poultice), comfrey (ointment or crushed leaves), dandelion (juice of stems and tea), elderberry juice, horseradish embrocation, hyssop, mint, parsley and yarrow. Oils made with balm, bay, lavender, marjoram, rosemary and thyme are good for rubbing into painful areas.

Sunburn
Ointments of elderflowers, marigold flowers; compresses of angelica, elderflowers and salad burnet. For other burns, apply oil of lavender or peppermint.

HERBS IN COSMETICS

Herbs of all varieties have long been used for cosmetic purposes – they were all that was available before the foundation of the commercial cosmetic industry. It is only recently that the properties of many plant sources are being re-evaluated and, with some doubts being expressed about the preservative chemicals used in commercial preparations, the age-old remedies are regaining their popularity and justified place in everyday life.

Home-made herbal cosmetics are economical, fun to experiment with and are, for the most part, purer and as effective as commercial products. However, it should not need to be emphasized that, however much herbal remedies are used, they cannot be effective if the diet and lifestyle remain unchanged: a yarrow face mask can do little for a spotty complexion if what has contributed internally to those spots is being ignored; a rosemary hair rinse will not make hair shine if the hair's dullness is due to poor diet. It has become a cliché that "beauty comes from an inner health", but we *are* what we eat and do, and fried foods, an excess of sugar, too little fresh fruit and vegetables, late nights and stress can all affect general health and therefore the look of the skin, hair, eyes and every part of the body.

By following a good and healthy diet, and by using herbs in cookery or in teas and tisanes – thus taking internal advantage of their beneficial essential oils – an external use of herbal preparations can be made more effective and can amplify that effect. If you are using yarrow, for instance, to counteract a greasy skin, it will also be good to actually eat yarrow leaves and drink yarrow as a tea as well. But, like many other things, herbs and flowers can cause allergic reactions. If you think you might be allergic to something, do a "patch" test first. Apply a little of the solution behind your ear and leave for about an hour. If the skin has turned red or has become swollen you should not use that herb cosmetically.

Herbal remedies are various: they can benefit the skin of the body when used in the bathwater; they can tone, moisturize, and cleanse the facial skin; they can improve the growth, colour, and condition of the hair; and they can help relieve aching eyes. Do remember, though, that herb remedies don't last: make up creams in small quantities. When dried and made into herb pillows or sachets and pot-pourri (see page 19), they

can induce the sleep that is so vital to general health and beauty.

Herbs in the Bath

Baths are taken primarily for cleansing but they can also be relaxing and stimulating. A warm soak at bedtime is considered by many people to be essential for sound sleep; conversely, many find a bath refreshing and stimulating, a necessity to wake the body up at the beginning of the day. In general, baths are good for the skin, for water is a beauty preparation in itself – it is, after all, a major component of the skin. The warmth and steam of a bath will open the pores, easing cleaning, and will stimulate the circulation – an effect magnified when taking a facial sauna (see below). If herbs are added to that water, they give not only fragrance, but many of their oils directly benefit the skin.

There are several ways of adding herbs to the bath. Fresh leaves or flowers can be scattered onto the hot water while it is running (but this can be messy, and rosemary, say, could be uncomfortable to sit on!). Strong infusions of a herb could be added to the bathwater. Several drops of a strong herb oil (home-made, see page 22, or essential oil available from herbalists' stores and often from aromatherapists), can be added to the water in exactly the same way as proprietory bath oils; as could some herb vinegars. And you can make up a little muslin or cheesecloth bag of the chosen herb – or a variety – and hang it from the hot tap so that the bathwater runs through it; the same little bag actually steeped in the water while you're in it (rather like a bath bouquet garni!) will be rather less messy than a scattering of herbs (a lidded tea strainer could serve the same purpose).

Many herbs can be used in the bathwater, and can claim to have individual benefits. Here are a few suggestions.

Soothing, Relaxing and Sedative
Balm, chamomile, lavender, marjoram, peppermint, rosemary, valerian.

Cleansing
A spring mixture of dandelions, nettles and other wild herbs, chamomile, lovage.

Tonic
Marjoram, nettles.

Stimulating
Angelica, elderflowers, thyme.

Improving Skin
Peppermint, marigold flowers, sage, salad burnet, yarrow.

Facial "Saunas"
This is a thorough, deep-cleansing treatment which is beneficial to all types of skin excepting only perhaps delicate dry skins and those with broken veins or capillaries or severe acne. It is particularly good for oily or greasy skins with blemishes such as spots or blackheads. It should be used only about once a week, or slightly more frequently if the skin is really oily. The skin must first be immaculately cleaned.

Infuse the chosen herb – fresh or dried – in a large bowl of boiling water. Lean over the bowl with a towel over your head to enclose the steam. Don't get any closer than about 12in/30cm. Steam the face for about 20 minutes, and this would be a good time – but carefully – to squeeze any blackheads. Dab the face afterwards with a skin tonic, followed perhaps by a mask, to close the pores (see below). Do not go out for at least an hour after the treatment.

Many herbs are beneficial, but the following are generally related to specific conditions. The herbs can also be used in a mixture, and an essential oil could be used in the boiling water instead of the herb.

Stimulating and Cleansing
Elderflowers, lavender, lime flowers, nasturtium, peppermint, rosemary, salad burnet, thyme.

Healing
Chamomile, comfrey, fennel.

Antiseptic
Lime flowers, peppermint.

For Greasy Skin
Yarrow.

Astringent
Sage.

Face Packs or Masks
These are an ancient form of beauty treatment and leave all types of skin soft, glowing and fresh. Dry skins, however, require a certain amount of care. Almost anything could be used to perform a specific beautifying purpose, but bases of natural yogurt or egg whites are the simplest and most effective. To these simply add some

finely chopped herb of choice, or a little of a cold, strong herbal decoction. Spread the paste onto the clean facial skin, avoiding the lips and eye area (you could cover your eyes with pads soaked in fennel or eyebright water to enjoy a simultaneous eye treatment), and then relax for about 10-15 minutes. Try to avoid laughing, talking or frowning while the pack is hardening as this will crack it, and will be rather uncomfortable! Rinse off carefully with lukewarm water and pat dry before moisturizing.

Many of the herbs already mentioned above can be used in face packs; they have many of the same properties when used in packs – being astringent, tonic, stimulating and cleansing. Greasy skins benefit particularly from yarrow, chamomile flowers, parsley, nettle, peppermint and sage. For dry skins, the yogurt base only should be used (the egg white is too drying), and a thin coating of oil could be applied before the pack: use comfrey, fennel, marigold flowers, borage, coltsfoot, lady's mantle, salad burnet and elderflowers. An ageing skin can benefit from packs made of sage, chamomile, yarrow, peppermint, and fennel. The latter is reputed to iron out wrinkles but, sadly, it's only temporary!

Herbal Cleansers and Lotions
Cleansers can be made from either herb oils (see page 22), or from any plain unscented cold cream. Chop the fresh herb of choice finely and add to cold cream; or melt a little cold cream and add some essential oil, some home-made herb oil or a little of a strong herb decoction. Cleansing lotions can be strong individual infusions, or can be infusions with a little added herb vinegar, for well diluted vinegar is good for the skin (see page 23).

Herbs that are beneficial are violet flowers, lady's mantle, chamomile flowers, elderflowers, lime flowers, rosemary, sage, salad burnet, eyebright, nettle, comfrey, peppermint, fennel and yarrow.

Use a herbal rinse – rosemary or sage – to enhance dark hair.

Skin Tonics and Fresheners
Cleansing should always be followed by the application of a skin tonic to "tone" the skin, to help close the pores, and to remove the last traces of cleanser. Tonics are simply made from strong infusions, and a well diluted herb vinegar can occasionally be used on a very oily skin – but it is strong in effect, and can over-dry.

Choose from the following, which have extra benefits.

For Wrinkles
Fennel, lime flowers, lemon balm, chamomile.

To Slightly Bleach (and remove freckles)
Parsley, elderflowers, lady's mantle.

For Broken Veins or Capillaries
Chamomile, coltsfoot, yarrow.

For Greasy Skin or Spots
Comfrey, coriander, elderflowers, marigold flowers, parsley, rose, rosemary, sage, yarrow.

To Tone
Dandelions, fennel, geranium, lavender, marigold, mint, nettle, rose.

To Heal
Chamomile, comfrey, rosemary.

Moisturizers
Even the most oily skin needs a thin film of moisturizer to protect it – especially after a thorough cleansing and toning. Simply add a little of a herbal infusion to a plain unscented moisturizing cream; melt the cream slightly and stir in the infusion. Good herbs to use are fennel, comfrey, lady's mantle and elderflowers – the best being salad burnet which tones, refines and softens the skin all in one.

For the Eyes
The eyes quickly reflect the general health of the body – dull when you're tired or unwell, bright and sparkling when you're fit. Puffiness, minor infections such as conjunctivitis, dark circles and eyestrain are all believed to be helped by certain herbs. Instead of using a proprietory eye bath, soak little pads of lint or cotton wool in a cold herb infusion, place them over your eyes, and lie down for 10 minutes or so; or, if the herb is already made up into teabags, these are almost tailor-made for the purpose!

The most effective herbs to use are eyebright (the best, not surprisingly, in view of its name), fennel, verbena, elderflowers, chamomile flowers, rue, rosehip, oregano, coltsfoot, lovage, rosemary, sage, savory and mint.

For the Hair
Hair, like eyes, is quick to mirror inner health. Hair is also subject to the dryness and greasiness that affects skin, and can be damaged by over-heating, and the harsh chemicals in some shampoos. In fact, most shampoos – which are basically detergents – can stand a certain amount of dilution without diminishing their cleansing powers, and this is an ideal way in which to add the benefits of herbs: simply make a strong infusion of your favourite herb and add a cupful to your shampoo. The best herbs for this purpose are rosemary and sage (for dark hair), chamomile (for fair hair), parsley and nettles (to prevent dandruff; rosemary is good too), and yarrow (for greasy hair).

To condition the hair, you can use an appropriate herb oil (see page 22). Massage the scalp with it once a week; leave it on the hair for as long as possible, covered with a hot damp towel, then shampoo off thoroughly.

To thoroughly clean the hair after shampooing, give it a final rinse with a herbal infusion. Pour it over the head into a bowl so that it can be re-used several times. Dark hair will benefit from a diluted herb vinegar – see page 23 – or a rosemary infusion. A sage rinse will darken greying hair. A chamomile infusion and some lemon juice will make fair hair shine. Marigold petals are conditioning for all kinds of hair too, and lemon verbena and lavender will give hair a wonderful fragrance.

IDENTIFYING HERBS

In this section, the most common culinary herbs are identified visually, with notes on their traditional usages in cookery. There are also guidelines on how to cultivate them, as well as a brief introduction to their medicinal and cosmetic benefits.

Angelica
(Angelica archangelica)

Angelica is a large, good-looking plant with the "umbrella" head of flowers typical of the *umbelliferae* family (which includes chervil, coriander, lovage and parsley). The whole plant is scented, and its strong stems are hollow. Although most of it can be eaten – the leaves in salads and the roots and stems cooked as vegetables – angelica is best known today as a candied or crystallized stem used for decorating cakes, trifles and other puddings. These stems should preferably be gathered in late spring and early summer, before the plant flowers. The freshly shredded leaves are a good flavouring for rhubarb, and can be used in jam-making, particularly sour jams; they help to reduce the need for sugar in such tart fruits as rhubarb, plums and gooseberries. Add them to compotes of fruit as well. A syrup can be made from the stems and leaves which, diluted, makes a refreshing – and healthy – drink. Angelica, once an antidote to spells and witchcraft, is now used in the making of Chartreuse and other liqueurs.

Medicinal

The name angelica is said to derive from an angel who visited a monk in a dream and told him the plant would cure the plague. Perhaps this is why it has been associated throughout the ages with curing many other ailments, among them coughs, colds and colic. (A root held in the mouth was also considered good for the relief of flatulence.) Angelica can be made into a tea to calm and release tension (it tastes rather like China tea), and the dried leaves are a good addition to pot-pourri.

Cultivation

Angelica, a biennial, can grow to more than 2m (6ft) high, and makes a striking backdrop to a herb garden. Cultivated in French herb gardens particularly, it can also be found as an "escape" in the wild. Stems and leaves are a light green, and yellow-green flowers appear in umbels in the summer. Plant seeds in early autumn or spring in a partially shady position with humus-rich soil. Thin as soon as the seedlings are large enough to handle. Plants usually die after flowering and setting seed, but if the flower heads are nipped off, the plant and its stems will live longer and grow stronger. Once a few plants are established, they will self-seed if a few heads are retained.

Balm or Lemon Balm

(Melissa officinalis)

A favourite of bees as well as of beekeepers – who used it to increase the honey harvest (indeed the generic name *melissa* means bee) – balm, or bee-plant as it is often known, used to be planted around orchards to encourage pollination. It was the essential ingredient of Paracelsus' *elixir vital*, concocted to make man immortal, but nowadays balm gives its essence to Chartreuse and Benedictine, those potent liqueurs made by monks, who keep most of the other ingredients a secret. Balm is associated with happiness and merry-making, thus the fresh lemon-scented leaves and small white flowers are traditional – and delicious – in white wine cups; they're also good in a German claret cup made with cucumber, orange and soda water, and some leaves added to China tea or fruit juices give an intriguing flavour. A few freshly picked leaves can go into a green salad, into sauce for fish, or into stuffing for lamb or pork. Because of its delicate but distinctive lemon flavour, balm can be used fairly lavishly, often in place of lemon or lemon grass in some recipes. It can also be dried.

Medicinal

Balm is an old and highly valued medicinal plant, chiefly associated with its ability to induce relaxation, banish melancholy and to benefit the heart. It was one of Hippocrates' 400 simples, and even today "melissa" tea is a favourite of French herbalists, who prescribe it as a remedial tonic for headaches, depression and tiredness. Infused as a tea or tisane, it is also thought to be good for colic, cramps, fever, stomach ulcers and, because of its mildness, it is particularly effective for use with younger children. It can be used in pot pourri.

Cultivation

Balm, a shrubby perennial, grows to between 60cm and 1.2m (2–4ft) tall, and likes a rich, moist and well-drained soil in full sun. It has spearmint-shaped leaves which are soft to the touch and yield their scent immediately. Although the seeds take time to germinate (plant in the autumn or early spring), once established they grow easily and spread by root runners, therefore they need occasional pruning back: this also encourages new young growth. Balm can be grown successfully in a window box or pots. It is susceptible to frost, so it should be cut back in the autumn to just above ground level, and protected by straw in a hard winter.

Basil

(Ocimum basilicum)

Sweet basil, so essential to the distinctive flavours associated with the Mediterranean, has large, tender leaves that bruise easily and smell sweetly of cloves. It should be picked young and eaten raw, or almost so, since the aroma and flavour are elusive. Basil has a great affinity with tomatoes – use it lavishly on tomato salad – as well as with aubergines, courgettes and marrow. In the south of France, a few chopped leaves are sometimes thrust into a dish of a ratatouille just before serving. The famous pesto alla Genevese – basil and pine nut paste – is one of the greatest spaghetti sauces, and *soupe au pistou* would be no more than an ordinary vegetable soup if it were not for the "pommade" made with oil, garlic and basil pounded together and added to the bowl at the last moment. Fresh basil is also delicious with mozzarella cheese, potato salad or on a salad of dried haricot beans, and with rabbit and chicken.

It is quite simple to preserve basil. Push the leaves into a jar, sprinkle a little salt between the layers, and fill the jar with olive oil. Both leaves (which become black) and oil are good and carry the flavour into whatever they are added to. Basil can also be preserved by deep-freezing, after a brief blanching. Commercially dried basil is useful for making a winter version of pesto sauce, but the flavour of dried basil – more curry-like – can never compare with that of the freshly picked herb.

Medicinal

In the past, pots of basil were kept indoors both for culinary purposes and to keep flies away; it has even been suggested that eating a lot of basil can help repel mosquitoes. Basil is chiefly associated, however, with its sedative properties, and basil tea can combat flatulence, ease a cough and stimulate perspiration to reduce a fever. Generally basil is thought to be a good diuretic and to give relief from menstrual cramps, from insomnia and migraine, and, as a dried snuff, to clear nasal congestion. Because of its strong scent, it can be infused in hot water and inhaled to clear a stuffy head.

Cultivation

Common or sweet basil is an annual which can grow to a height of about 60cm (2ft). It has large dark green leaves, and white flowers in late summer. Sow seeds in the early spring indoors in a pot or in a greenhouse; basil requires warmth, as well as a light, well-drained soil. Do not over-water. Plant out in the early summer, after an initial hardening off. As the plant grows, nip out the flowers to promote foliage growth. Bring plants indoors in the autumn. There is also a bush basil (*basilicum minimum*) which grows only to about 25cm (10in) high, and a wild basil found occasionally growing in chalk or limestone; the former has as good a flavour as sweet basil; the latter is mild.

Bay
(*Laurus nobilis*)

Even the most basic cook is familiar with the sweet, resinous smell of bay. An amazingly versatile herb, bay leaves and twigs go into court-bouillon for fish, into stocks, broths and marinades, pickles and stews, daubes and spaghetti sauces – into everything, in fact, that demands a bouquet garni, of which it is a basic constituent. A fresh bay leaf is the best decoration for a terrine, and in the past bay leaves were used to flavour milk puddings – bay infused in boiled milk gives a very agreeable flavour, much nicer than synthetic vanilla. Pick leaves as needed, but bay is stronger when dried, and avoid buying old bay leaves: if they are more than a year old they will have lost their flavour as well as their colour. In France bay leaves are called *laurier,* dangerously translated as laurel leaves in many French cookbooks. It is only the leaves of the sweet laurel – bay leaves – that are suitable for human consumption.

As befits its name, the *laurus nobilis* has always represented glory and triumph, culminating in the "laurels" of success, the wreaths of bay leaves with which the ancient Greeks and Romans adorned the heads of their achievers. It was also thought to be a protective plant, and branches were hung in houses and over doors to both protect against disease and ill fortune, and to freshen. The ancient Greeks would burn the leaves as incense – and bay leaves added to the barbecue coals – or to kebabs to be barbecued – add a wonderful flavour.

Medicinal
Bay is related to cinnamon and camphor and thus its strong essential oils are effective against a variety of complaints. Although it is from its use in cooking that most of its benefits derive, it can also be used occasionally in natural medical treatments. It promotes sweating, so a decoction of leaves and boiling water can be drunk or inhaled as a remedy for flu and other fevers. A few leaves in a hot bath will help relieve aches and pains, and the mild inhalation involved will also aid infections such as bronchitis and tonsillitis. An oil in which the leaves have been steeped can be used warm as an aromatic rub for sore backs. Bay can also be added to pot-pourri.

Cultivation
The members of the laurel family are evergreen shrubs and the sweet laurel or bay can grow to upwards of 4.5–6m (15–20ft) high. The leaves are shiny, smooth and dark, and both male and female plants have inconspicuous yellow-green flowers in the spring, and the female plants thereafter bear long purplish berries. Plant seeds in early to mid spring in ordinary garden soil in a sunny position, or in potting compost in a tub – but small trees can be readily bought, and autumn cuttings can be taken from lateral shoots. When winters are likely to be cold, bay trees in tubs should be brought indoors.

Borage

(Borago officinalis)

Borage is one of the traditional herb-garden plants, but it also grows in the wild. It is a hairy, bristly plant, its name coming from the Latin *burra* meaning rough or shaggy hair or garment. The hairs on the leaves sting the fingers, but borage makes up for the discomfort it inflicts by its flowers, which are a heart-breaking blue and which, together with the cucumber flavour of both leaves and flowers, complete that fruit-salad of an English summer drink called Pimms. A soup can be made from borage leaves – a cool green colour which can be enhanced by a blue borage flower floating in the middle – and the leaves can also be added to other soups for flavour, and be cooked as a vegetable like spinach. The tender tops and the flowers can be added to summer salads – the flowers making a particularly pretty decoration for crab salad. The flowers can be candied for decorating cakes, desserts and ice cream, and dried to add colour to pot-pourri.

Medicinal

I, Borage
Bring alwaies courage

This couplet, thought to be coined by Pliny, pops up in every herbal and treatise on herbs, revealing borage's most consistent medicinal virtue – that of instilling courage as well as happiness. Indeed it is thought to be nature's "pep" pill, and a drug derived from borage is used by French homeopathic doctors to treat depression, fevers and nervous disorders. Borage tea is exhilarating and is food for the heart and the blood; infusions of the leaves and flowers are good for catarrh. The leaves contain a substance also found in human breast milk which may explain why borage is believed to stimulate the breast-milk flow.

Cultivation

Borage is a tall annual – from 45–90cm (1½–3ft), a height which it can reach very quickly – with hollow stems, corrugated leaves with grey bristles, and pendent star-shaped blue flowers from early sumemr to autumn (although pink and white flowers are also known). Borage can grow in most garden soils and sites although it prefers a well-drained, sunny position. Plant seed in spring and thin to 30cm (12in) apart when the seedlings are large enough to handle. The plants will be fully grown in about eight weeks, and they are self seeding. Do not plant in pots.

Chervil

(Anthriscus cerefolium)

Chervil is one of the classic *fines herbes,* and its delicate and refreshing aniseedy flavour complements and improves the flavour of other herbs with which it is combined. It has been grown in Europe – for both its culinary and medicinal properties – since Roman times, and indeed the French often use it in place of the omnipresent parsley, even for garnishing. It does in fact rather resemble parsley, although it is more delicate and fern-like. Because the flavour of chervil is subtle, it needs to be used lavishly, and thus it is useful to have several plants in the garden.

It is good in green salads, with eggs, with sauces (Béarnaise particularly), and as a herb butter for steak or sole. In Korea it is used as a salad instead of lettuce, served by itself or with a dish of grilled or curried prawns. It makes a delicious quiche with Emmental cheese, and a very good light soup – perhaps its best use, and one which is very popular on the Continent – and chervil and sorrel, both shredded fairly finely, are a traditional garnish for chicken soup. Chervil can be bought canned, and fresh chervil can be frozen, but it doesn't dry very well.

Medicinal

Chervil is best in spring; its leaves are blood-cleansing and diuretic; and the juice of the leaves also has internal and external cleansing properties. All these combine to make chervil one of the more popular Lenten herbs of history. As it increases the perspiration, it is beneficial when eaten during fevers and similar illnesses. Finely chopped and warmed chervil can be applied to bruises and aching joints to relieve pain.

Cultivation

Chervil is a hardy biennial herb with ridged aromatic stems and bright green and ferny leaves (which can be both smooth or curly); white flowers in umbels appear from early to late summer in the plant's second year. It grows to a height of about 30–45cm (12–18in) and, with successive sowings, can be picked virtually at any time of the year (but cover the plants in a severe winter). It flourishes in all soils except a very wet and heavy one, and can be grown in window boxes and containers. Sow seed from early spring to late summer in partial shade, and thin finally to about 30cm (12in) apart. Leaves can be picked after about eight weeks, and if the seeds are not required, pinch out the flower heads as soon as they appear.

Chives

(Allium schoenoprasum)

Chives are the smallest member of the onion family, and are invaluable in the kitchen. They were not cultivated in Britain until the Middle Ages – nor in America until European settlers arrived there – but had been used in China for their culinary and medicinal properties at least 5,000 years ago.

With a flavour faintly redolent of onions but far finer and more delicate, chives are best with eggs, especially omelettes, with potatoes – particularly baked potatoes split open and piled with soured cream mixed with chopped chives – and with raw or cooked tomatoes. As they are such a clean, fresh green they look pretty, cut up small with scissors to prevent them bruising, sprinkled over puréed soups (tomato, vichyssoise, avocado, potato or artichoke), in a lettuce salad and as a garnish for potato salad and glazed carrots. They are used in the classic *fines herbes,* and are chopped to use in sauce tartare and chive butter. The tiny bulbs can be pickled like small onions. As the flavour is destroyed by long cooking, chives should be added to a dish at the last moment. Chives freeze well, but do not dry.

Medicinal

The Chinese used chives medicinally as an antidote to poisoning and a remedy for bleeding. As the members of the onion family in general have antiseptic properties, so too do chives to a lesser degree. They are also known to stimulate the appetite, to be digestive (even for those who find onions difficult to cope with), and are diuretic, thus helping kidney function. They are rich in iron, so are good for the blood and diseases involving the blood, and are particularly useful in invalid cookery.

Cultivation

A hardy, perennial herb, chives have a minute bulb, and grass-like tubular leaves which grow to a height of about 25cm (10in). Dense globular pink flowers appear in the summer (beloved of flower arrangers despite their faint onion fragrance, as they dry well), but these should be nipped off before flowering to encourage leaf growth. Sow seeds in early spring or early summer in a rich soil in full or partial sun and thin seedlings to about 15cm (6in) apart. To ensure a continual supply of leaves through the summer, cut back the leaves several times to 5–7.5cm (2–3in) during the growing season, water them well, and fertilize in autumn and early spring. Divide clumps every two or three years and replant 15cm (6in) apart. They can also be grown successfully in pots.

Coriander
(Coriandrum sativum)

Coriander could be one of the oldest flavourings – both spice and herb – as it is mentioned in many ancient texts from around the world, and it is one of the bitter herbs designated in the Bible to be eaten at Passover. The soft floppy leaves – which look rather like lacy, flat parsley – have a strong smell when crushed which is quite unlike the warm flavour of the seeds. But until the seeds ripen, the young plant has an unpleasant smell, said to be similar to that of bed-bugs (indeed the name coriander comes from the Greek word for bed-bug)!

Coriander is used to good effect in many of the world's cuisines: the Chinese claim it as their own, calling it Chinese parsley; it is frequently used in Mexico, where it flourishes; Moroccan souks are heady with its scent; and it is also popular in the Middle East, Africa, Asia and southern Spain. The seeds are a major ingredient in curry powder, and the leaves are an essential flavour in many types of curry, particularly prawn and mutton; the most flavourful use of the leaves is in an Indian coriander chutney, a paste made from fresh ginger, garlic, green chilli and fresh coriander, all pounded together. Coriander also lends a superb flavour, used sparingly, to meatballs, lamb stews, and lamb or pork kebabs. The leaves do not dry well, but can be frozen or preserved with salt in oil; dry the seeds.

Medicinal

One of the simples of Hippocrates, over the centuries coriander has been considered to be a love potion, an aphrodisiac, a cure for dizziness and colic, and a narcotic. It has been used as a herb for beauty: an infusion of the leaves can diminish skin redness and spots. So highly aromatic are the seeds that they were once used as a preservative, being rubbed into meat to keep it fresh. The seeds were also used by druggists to mask the flavour of unpleasant medicine and by distillers to lend warmth to their wares.

Cultivation

The herb coriander has become increasingly familiar in the West through the bunches, roots intact, available from ethnic grocery shops. But it is an easy plant to grow, and the flavour of the home-grown seeds or herb is infinitely superior to shop-bought. It is an annual and can grow to a height of 60cm (2ft). It has bright green deeply indented leaves which are like flat parsley at the base of the plant and feathery at the top; mauve umbels of flowers appear in the summer and set to seed later in the season. Sow seed in early spring in light rich soil in full sun. Germination can be slow. Thin out the seedlings to about 10-15cm (4-6in) apart. Cut the leaves as needed and harvest the seeds when they are a light grey-brown.

Dill

(Anethum graveolens)

Dill, like coriander and fennel, can be used both as herb and spice; all parts of the plant are aromatic, with a sharp but sweet aniseed taste, the leaves being gentler in flavour than the seeds. As both spice and herb it is particularly popular in northern Europe. The Scandinavians, for instance, are as fond of dill as they are of summer, the height of which is the first day of the *krefta* season, when thousands of crayfish are cooked with quantities of dill, served in their scarlet shells on a bed of green dill and accompanied by numerous glasses of akvavit, interspersed with beer. Dill is the flavour that makes Scandinavian pickled salmon *(gravlax)* so delicious, and is used as a matter of course with boiled and mashed potatoes. Dill is also used to add its inimitable flavour to pickled fish, to baby cucumbers or gherkins – known as dill pickles in the USA – and thus to vinegars. It is particularly good with vegetables and fish; with white fish serve dill either in melted butter or made into a sauce rather like parsley sauce. The leaves can be scattered in a salad (cucumber is a good partner), and it can be blended with cream or cottage cheese for a tasty sandwich filling. To preserve dill, freeze it in plastic bags, or use dried dill seeds when fresh dill is out of season.

Medicinal

The word dill comes from a Saxon word meaning "to lull", and dill, because of its soothing effect, is used in digestive potions for babies; it is both gentle and effective against colic and other minor stomach ailments. It also induces sleep in babies, and a cup of dill tea last thing at night is no less efficacious for adults! Dill seeds were known as "Meeting House" seeds, eaten in the New World during long sermons to prevent people from feeling hungry; they were also chewed to sweeten the breath.

Cultivation

Dill is a hardy annual, of the same family as fennel, and can grow to a height of 90cm (3ft). It has feathery green-blue foliage, and tiny yellow flowers in umbels appear throughout the summer. Dill likes sunny, well-drained sites, but it must never be allowed to go short of water or the plant will not develop properly. Sow seed in its permanent position in successive monthly sowings from early spring to early summer, and thin when seedlings are large enough to handle. Dill seeds itself very successfully, and it can be grown in pots although pot plants will never achieve the same size as the ones in the garden.

Fennel
(Foeniculum vulgare)

The sweet herb fennel – not to be confused with the bulbous vegetable Florence fennel – is used both as a herb and for its seeds. It has a uniquely sweet anise flavour, which is contained in all parts of the plant apart from the root: the stems, for instance, can be cooked and eaten rather like celery or asparagus, a usage to which the Romans put the plant. Fennel has long been associated with fish cookery – indeed it is sometimes called the "fish herb". A few small twigs are invaluable for bouillabaisse, bourride and with sardines, and if you catch your own crayfish try cooking them in boiling water with a mass of fennel; it gives them a most delicate flavour and is a good alternative to dill. Burn a few dried twigs when you are grilling fish or lamb outdoors, and put twigs inside a fish and under it when you bake it in the oven. The anise-flavoured oils permeate the food with a wonderfully sympathetic flavour. Sprigs can also be added to salads, soups and to cooked vegetables, and they make a delicate and delicious garnish. In Sardinia, wild fennel is often used to flavour a bean and pork stew, and occasionally lamb. Preserve fennel leaves as dill; dry the seeds.

Medicinal
Fennel's relationship with fish is due to its ability to counteract the less digestible fats of oily fish; it is also consistently reputed to be able to help fat people lose weight. Its digestive properties are used, like dill, in colic remedies for babies. But its principal medicinal and cosmetic benefits are for the eyes: compasses of cold fennel tea work wonders on inflamed or watery eyes, and were once even thought to improve the eyesight. If applied as a cosmetic face pack, fennel is also credited with the ability to reduce wrinkles.

Cultivation
A hardy perennial, fennel can grow to more than 1.8m (6ft) in height. Like dill, it has feathery blue-tinged foliage, and tiny yellow flowers appear in umbels in the summer. Fennel likes a moist, well-drained soil in full sun, but grows well in a variety of conditions. Sow seed in late winter and early spring and thin later. Pluck out flower heads as they form unless seeds are to be harvested. Established plants can be divided in spring. Fennel grows heartily in the wild, and is also happy in large containers.

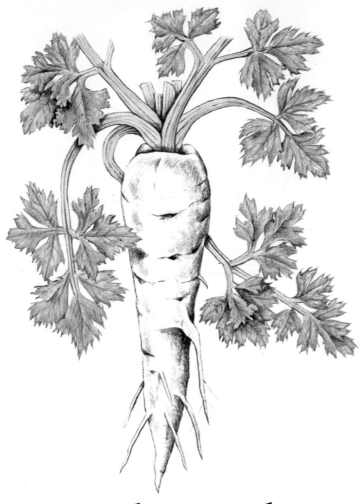

Hamburg Parsley

(Carum petroselinum fusiformis)

Hamburg parsley – a variety of parsley with a parsnip-like root – arrived in Britain at the beginning of the 18th century. It originated in Europe where it had been appreciated for centuries, both for its roots which can be cooked as a vegetable (like celeriac in texture, like a mild celery in flavour), and for its leaves which, parsley-like in look and flavour, were valued in winter when the more common herb parsley could not survive.

As its name might suggest, Hamburg parsley is most popular in eastern and northern Europe: the Poles and Russians use it as a pot herb along with carrots and onions, in stews, casseroles and soups. It could replace parsnips in recipes where it will have a much less strident effect; it could be cooked as an accompanying vegetable like celeriac, and it could be cut into chips and deep-fried. The young leaves, though edible, are coarser and of poorer flavour than the common herb parsley.

Medicinal

Parsley roots and seeds were mentioned often in European pharmacopoeias, and were associated in general with curing malarial disorders. The roots that are eaten as a vegetable were believed to have a beneficial effect on the kidneys. But there are few folk remedies attached to Hamburg parsley, although many of the attributes of common parsley may also apply to its rooted cousin.

Cultivation

Hamburg parsley is hardy. Sow seeds in shallow drills 30cm (12in) apart from early to mid spring, in soil that is well drained and fertile, preferably enriched with manure or compost. Thin seedlings to 20cm (8in) apart, and water the plants well throughout the summer. The roots need a long growing season, to develop properly – the biggest are the best – so they should not be harvested until at least the middle of the autumn as required for cooking. They can be left in the ground all winter, but it is better and safer to lift them in late autumn and store them, as any other winter vegetable.

Horseradish
(Armoracia rusticana)

The most pungent of all cultivated roots, horseradish is a native of southwestern Europe, and grows wild in Britain, all over mainland Europe, North America and New Zealand. It has an ancient history – the Egyptians and Romans, both renowned for their appreciation of strong tastes, grew it – and it was referred to by Dioscorides. Both the root and the leaves were used, and the leaves – which we now consider inedible – were one of the bitter herbs eaten during Passover.

A fresh stinging horseradish sauce with roast beef is one of life's pleasures, and is very good, too, with hot boiled tongue. In Germany, horseradish is grated and mixed with vinegar as a sauce for fish; it can be mixed with mayonnaise as a dressing for hard-boiled eggs; or with cream, yogurt or soured cream to make a sauce for meats or vegetables (a potato/yogurt/horseradish salad is particularly good). As it loses its pungency quickly when cooked, it is most often used raw. It can be grated and stored in vinegar in a screw-top jar for a hottish pickle (the vinegar is tasty thereafter too). A few gratings can be mixed in with puréed vegetables like turnip or beetroot, or with coleslaw. Commercial dried horseradish flakes are a reasonable substitute for the fresh root.

Medicinal
Pliny considered horseradish an extremely healthful plant, and it has since been considered to be good for the stomach, and for the sinuses – as the aroma when peeling or grating it is stronger than the strongest onion, even the most blocked nose is cleared! Its reputation as an anti-scorbutic – preventing scurvy – is more scientifically based on its rich content of vitamin C. The heat of the root, when mixed with an oil or the yolk of an egg, can be used to great effect as an embrocation on aching muscles or joints, sciatica and chilblains.

Cultivation
Horseradish is a hardy perennial, the floppy green leaves of which can reach a height of 60cm (2ft). It is very easy to grow; indeed it is less easy to prevent it from spreading and taking over the entire garden. It thrives wild all over wasteland, commons and on railway cuttings, and the best way to grow it is from dug or bought roots or "thongs" of about 20cm (8in) long. Plant these in good soil in a sunny position about 30cm (12in) apart, and they will soon sprout if well watered. They can be lifted for use or storage in the autumn. Dig over the bed thereafter to prevent it spreading.

Lovage
(Levisticum officinale)

An old-fashioned herb which looks rather like immensely tall celery that has got out of hand, with a very strange, though pleasant heavy smell. It is called the Maggi plant in Holland because the flavour is reminiscent of stock cubes, with monosodium glutamate lurking somewhere in its nuances – a sort of yeasty cross between celery and curry. Lovage is a strong-flavoured herb, being noticeably more pungent than other herbs. Both the leaves and seeds can be used, but fairly sparingly, to season stocks and soups when a meaty flavour is required. Indeed a lovage tea is more like a broth, with salt a more natural seasoning than sugar. The leaves can be used to make a soup on their own (good with some orange juice added), in casseroles, or to give tang to stuffings or gravies; they can be added to salads or omelettes, mixed with mustard and butter for a seasoning for fish, and chopped into a cream or Hollandaise sauce. The young stalks can be eaten cooked as a vegetable in a white sauce, and they can also be candied like angelica. The leaves are best used fresh, but can be dried.

Medicinal

Lovage has often been associated with the passions but this has probably more to do with its name than any inherent aphrodisiac property. What it is generally reputed to do, though, is cleanse, both externally and internally, as well as deodorize. Lovage tea is good for the stomach and the digestion, and sprigs of lovage in the bathwater are good for the skin. A cold infusion relieves tired or red eyes. Lovage is also said to be antiseptic, with lovage poultices placed directly on wounds. It can be added, again sparingly, to pot-pourri.

Cultivation

Lovage is a vigorous perennial, and can grow up to 2m (7ft) in height. Its leaves most closely resemble those of celery, and it has yellow umbels of flowers in late summer. It prefers a rich moist soil, in a sunny position, and can stay happily in one position for a number of years. Seeds can be sown in spring (germination is slow), or the roots of existing plants can be divided in spring when the leaves start to emerge, or autumn.

Marjoram

(Origanum spp)

There are several varieties of marjoram – the sweet or knotted, the pot, and wild marjoram or oregano. SWEET MARJORAM (*Origanum majorana*) is also known as knotted marjoram because of the little knot-like bracts from which the clusters of flowers appear. It is generally considered to be the finest of the marjorams for culinary use, as it is milder in flavour. The whole plant smells very sweet, both when it is fresh, and when it is cut, just after flowering, and dried in bunches like thyme and sage. The flavour is spicy as well, and it is one of the constituents of bouquet garni. Basically a meat herb, marjoram is best used in made-up dishes or mixtures like meat loaf and home-made sausages. Similarly, it is very good in stuffings or forcemeats, the flavour coming through strongly; use it in stuffings for chicken, guinea fowl, rabbit or hare, and in the mixtures used to stuff vegetables. It is excellent with pulses, and dried, can be used in spaghetti and tomato sauces and any tomato-based soup or stew. Meats can be rubbed with fresh marjoram leaves before grilling or roasting, or mixed with other leaves in a salad. When dried, marjoram leaves have a strong aroma, and can be used successfully in pot-pourri. POT MARJORAM (*Origanum onites*) is slightly less warm flavoured than sweet marjoram, but can be used in exactly the same ways. In fact its name reveals its essential usefulness to the cook, as it can be grown indoors in a pot, providing leaves for winter use.

Medicinal

Marjoram was one of the strewing herbs in the 17th and 18th centuries – they were thrown over floors to disguise smells and to combat disease. These disinfectant and preservative properties were also of value when rubbed on meat in the days before refrigeration, and when added to sausage and other meat mixtures. Infusions of marjoram are believed to help infections of the mouth and toothache, and to be effective against sore throats and coughs. Dried and ground, it has been used as a snuff to help with nasal congestion. Marjoram steeped in oil, or warmed bunches of marjoram, are good for stiff and aching rheumatic joints.

Cultivation

SWEET MARJORAM, in all but the hottest climates, is a half-hardy annual. It is a pretty bush with red stems and small greyish green leaves, growing to between 30–60cm (1–2ft) in height; tubular white, pink or mauve flowers open from early to late summer. Seeds can be sown outdoors in mid to late spring in ordinary garden soil in a warm, sunny position; thin out when seedlings are large enough to handle. They can also be sown indoors in early spring; but the seedlings will need to be hardened off before planting outside later in the season, when all danger of frost is past. Sweet marjoram will grow happily in pots as well, to be taken inside in winter.

POT MARJORAM is a hardy dwarf shrub with oval bright green leaves, and mauve to white flowers on long stems in the summer. It grows to about 30cm (12in) in height. It is best propagated from heel cuttings taken in late spring, or from root division in early spring, but seeds can also be sown in light soil in a sheltered position at the same time of year. If in pots, pot marjoram can be kept out of doors, but will need to be taken indoors in winter – it is deciduous, so would lose its leaves if left outside.

Apple mint

Spearmint

Mint
(Mentha spp)

One of the oldest and most familiar of herbs, mint has almost as many varieties – there are over 40 – as it has uses. Legend has it that mint got its name from Menthe, a nymph beloved of Pluto, king of the underworld. Pluto's wife, Persephone, was so jealous that she turned Menthe into the herb which bears her name. Two varieties of mint are most commonly grown for kitchen use – spearmint and apple mint – but most of the other mints, especially those discussed below, can be used similarly.

In England mint is traditionally used as an accompaniment to roast lamb in mint sauce or jelly, but it is also very popular in the Middle East; finely chopped and stirred into yogurt it makes a dressing for cucumber salad; or it lends its unique flavour to the Lebanese salad of cracked wheat, *tabbouli*. In northern India, chopped mint is used in fresh chutney – mixed with fresh green chilli and yogurt it is very good with Tandoori chicken. Mint is often boiled with vegetables. It is virtually traditional with new potatoes and fresh garden peas, but it transforms other young vegetables such as carrots, green beans and parsnips. Fresh leaves can also be added to vegetable soups, and served with shellfish, notably prawns. Mint is particularly good when used in ice creams, sorbets and mousses, and in the making of puddings that contain fresh oranges (with which it has an affinity), or chocolate. Sprigs of fresh mint go into fruit drinks, wine cups and juleps (a chopped leaf transforms a cup of hot chocolate), and it makes the hot sweet mint tea so prevalent in Morocco. The mints can be dried; the best is spearmint.

SPEARMINT *(mentha spicata)* is the most commonly used in the kitchen. It has pointed smooth green leaves, and a fresh taste; it grows to a height of about 45cm (18in) and purplish flowers appear in autumn. It occasionally grows in the wild, but mainly as an escape, and it grows well in pots.

APPLE MINT *(mentha rotundifolia)* is much prettier than spearmint, with woolly, rounded leaves (the woolliness disappears when it is chopped). Its flavour is superior to that of spearmint, and the plant, as its name suggests, smells strongly of apples. It grows to a height of 60–90cm (2–3ft) or more, with reddish stems and purplish white flowers in the summer. It can be found in the wild on roadsides and waste land. It can be grown in containers but plants should be replaced every year.

PEPPERMINT *(mentha piperita)* is a hybrid, a cross between spearmint and water mint, and it is the oils from this mint primarily that are used to give a mint flavour to confectionery, toothpastes, chewing gum, hair tonic and indigestion remedies. It is also used in the making of liqueurs such as Crème de Menthe, Chartreuse and Benedictine. It grows to about 60cm (2ft) tall, and has reddish stems, dark green longish pointed leaves, and light purple flowers in autumn. It can be grown in a pot on its own. It is this mint which is most used medicinally.

PENNYROYAL *(mentha pulegium)* was once used to keep away fleas; its generic name comes from the Latin *pulex*, meaning flea. It is a tiny prostrate or creeping mint, growing to only 10–15cm (4–6in) tall; it has tiny green leaves and purple flowers in autumn. It is a good plant for window boxes and larger containers, but its best use is as a fragrant lawn or between paving stones, as it spreads easily and emits its wonderful minty fragrance when stepped on.

WATER MINT *(mentha aquatica)* is a wild mint found near swamps, marshes and river and lake banks. It grows up to 60cm (2ft) in height and has rough and hairy green leaves, often tinged with purple, and bluish lilac flowers from mid summer to the autumn. It is naturally very like peppermint in appearance, though its flavour is cleaner and more sharp.

CORN MINT *(mentha arvensis)* is also found in the wild, almost as commonly as water mint. It grows in arable fields, woods and damp places, up to a height of about 45cm (18in). Its leaves are soft, hairy and pale green – the plant is called lambs' tongues in Scotland because of their shape – and it has lilac flowers. Its flavour is coarser than the other mints.

BOWLES MINT *(mentha villosa alopecuroides)* looks like a larger version of apple mint; it can be used in similar ways.

HORSE MINT *(mentha longifolia)*, with long leaves as its Latin name suggests, grows wild beside streams, and is similar to a mild spearmint in flavour and smell.

EAU DE COLOGNE MINT *(mentha citrata)* is also known as orange mint because of its perfume and flavour – reminiscent of a cross between eau de Cologne and oranges.

Medicinal

The various mints have certain specific health properties in common, although peppermint is by far the most beneficial. The smell of mint has always been considered to be an encourager of the appetite, and the Romans would scour their tables with mint and strew it on the floor before feasts for that reason. Mint either eaten or taken as a tea calms the digestive tract, relieves cramps and colicky pains, and is a good stomach settler after vomiting or for morning sickness. This explains its use in indigestion remedies and in digestive after-meal teas. The oils of mint are antiseptic; peppermint oil in particular contains menthol which is used to ease headaches, neuralgic pains, bruises and toothache, having an almost analgesic action. Pots of pennyroyal were once taken on voyages so that sailors could purify their stale drinking water; pots taken indoors can repel insects (not just fleas, but mosquitoes, ants and flies as well). An infusion of mint is believed to be good for colds and coughs, as a general tonic, as a hangover cure, and a leaf chewed can variously prevent bad breath and cure hiccups!

Cultivation

As most mints are hybrid, they do not grow true from seed, so are best propagated by planting rooted pieces of the runners in well-dug ordinary garden soil; mint likes moisture but does equally well in a sunny or partially shaded position. As mint soon exhausts the soil, incorporate well-rotted compost or manure into the ground before planting, and replant root divisions every two years or so in early spring in a fresh position. Mint spreads like a weed so unless you want it to take over the herb garden (or indeed the *whole* garden), plant it in large bottomless containers sunk into the ground – old sinks or plastic buckets – or slot large roofing slates or tiles into the ground around where the mint is situated to contain the roots. This is one reason why mint is a good plant for window boxes and other containers.

Oregano
(Oreganum vulgare)

The name is derived from the Greek *oros*, a mountain, and *ganos*, joy, and it is often called locally "joy of the mountains". This wild marjoram has a wonderfully warm, heady scent and flavour. It is by far the strongest and spiciest of the marjorams, particularly when grown in hotter climates such as around the Mediterranean (where it probably originated), and in Mexico. It grows wild in northern Europe too, on chalk and limestone; it is common in England, Wales and southern Ireland, rarer in Scotland.

Oregano can be used in cooking in much the same way as the other marjorams, but as it is so much stronger, it should be used with discretion, particularly if dried, when it becomes sweeter. In Italy it is used for the same dishes as sweet marjoram, and it also adds its unique flavour to pizzas and spaghetti sauces, and to salads of mozzarella cheese and tomatoes. The dried leaves give a strong spicy flavour to an oil and lemon sauce for fish and roast meats, to chicken broth, beef stews and grilled fish, especially red mullet, and oregano is one of the flavours of the best chilli con carne, for it is used widely in Mexican cooking as well. *Rigani* is the wild marjoram of Greece – use the dried flowers rather than the leaves to give the authentic Greek flavour to lamb kebabs and the Greek salad of feta cheese, tomatoes, onions and olives. Olives steeped in oregano-flavoured olive oil take on the aroma of the herb, and the flowers and leaves added to a jar of sugar make a variation on the vanilla sugar theme.

Medicinal

As with basil, it has been suggested that eating a lot of oregano can help repel mosquitoes. Even smelling oregano frequently is believed to keep one in good health. Oregano has many of the medicinal attributes of the other marjorams, but it also contains further essential oils which make it very much more antiseptic in action, both internally and externally. Because of its heady scent, oregano – either in the garden or in a window box – is good for asthma and other respiratory disorders; the essential oil inhaled is good for the lungs. The marjoram sugar mentioned earlier is believed to be good for diseases of the kidneys and the eyes. Dried, oregano can be used in pot-pourri and in sleep pillows.

Cultivation

Oregano, a perennial, can grow to a height of some 45cm (18in). It has rounded, mid-green leaves, and tiny rose-purple flowers appear in the summer. Oregano can be grown from seed sown in spring, in the same sort of site as the other marjorams, or it can be propagated by division of roots in spring or autumn. It can also be grown in pots.

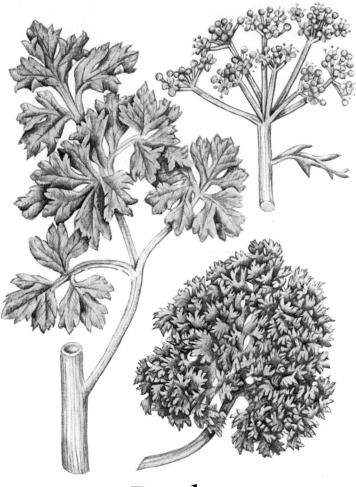

Parsley
(Petroselinum crispum)

Parsley is the most usable of herbs and one that you can always buy fresh, whether the curly-leafed type or the flat-leafed Continental parsley. It has been used for thousands of years, and is undoubtedly the most popular herb in European and American cookery. It is a constituent of a classic bouquet garni, one of the *fines herbes*, and it is the omnipresent garnishing sprig too often left at the side of the plate.

Parsley goes with almost any food. It seems to have just as much affinity with garlic and hard-flavoured Sicilian dishes, salty with olives, anchovies, goats' cheese and capers, as it does with the potato soups and fresh cod of the north, and many a dreary looking dish has been saved with a sprinkling of this chopped greenery. Flat-leafed parsley is tastier than the curled, and parsley roots – the roots of its cousin, Hamburg parsley – are good for flavouring stews. Use parsley in court-bouillons, soups and, of course, in parsley sauce. *Jambon persillé* – a dish of chunks of ham set in a jelly quite solid with green chopped parsley – is a Burgundian dish well worth trying. To make parsley sandwiches, wash and chop very finely some freshly gathered parsley, mix it with butter and spread thickly between two thin slices of brown bread; this parsley butter, spiked with garlic, is delicious with snails, mussels and many other plain fish and vegetable dishes. Deep-fried sprigs of parsley are a good garnish for fish.

Medicinal
The major medicinal benefit of parsley is that it is so highly nutritious. It contains large amounts of iron, calcium and other minerals and trace elements, as well as vitamins, C in particular: a sprig of parsley eaten per day could boost the C levels in the body and thus boost general good health, and keep colds at bay. It is a digestive, and is anti-flatulent and diuretic. Parsley tea is believed to help those who suffer from rheumatism. Chewing a parsley leaf is a classic way of sweetening the breath.

Cultivation
All varieties of parsley are biennial, they will over-winter successfully if covered – but they are best grown as annuals. They vary in height from tiny to 60cm (2ft) in height. A rich soil is needed, and the plant needs moisture, so a semi-shaded position is best. Sow seed in early spring either indoors or outdoors – where germination can take up to eight weeks. To hasten the process, soak the seeds overnight, or water them into the ground with hot water. Thin when the seedlings are large enough to handle, keep well weeded and watered, and feed occasionally to increase leaf production. In the second year cut off the flower stalks to delay seed production. Use as an edging plant in the herb garden, or grow in pots indoors for continual harvesting.

Rocket

(Eruca sativa)

This sadly ignored salad herb with its pale yellow flowers looks rather like mustard and has a slightly hot, peppery flavour which reveals its relationship to other members of the *cruciferae* or cabbage family (although one writer has surprisingly compared the flavour to fresh mushrooms). It grows wild throughout much of Europe, and cultivated varieties tend to be less stridently flavoured. It was approved of strongly by John Gerard, a herbalist writing in the 16th century – "a good salat-herbe" – but was later considered to be "fetid and offensive", which perhaps explains why it has disappeared from the salad bowls of England, along with many other salad greens like corn salad and purslane.

The young leaves of rocket give a dry aromatic taste to plain green salads and, chopped and mixed with spring onions, they can enliven tomato salads. In southern Italy – the country in which rocket enjoys its greatest popularity – the wild plant is used as an extra flavour in the mixed salads eaten with pasta or veal. But be careful which herb you use if plucking from the wild – the name rocket or its Continental equivalents applies to a number of other plants, some of them far too bitter to be eaten.

Medicinal

The principal recorded medicinal use of rocket is as a form of mild analgesic. Herbalists recommended that it be eaten to ease pain: one suggesting that it should be taken before a whipping, another that it would help when bitten by a shrew mouse "and other venomous beasts"!

Cultivation

Rocket grows 30–60cm (1–2ft) tall on long leafy stems, and has pale creamy-yellow flowers. It grows very easily from seed, and prefers a rich, moist soil although any ordinary garden soil will do. Sow seeds in short rows throughout the summer and thin the seedlings out to about 20cm (8in) apart when they are large enough to handle. The leaves will be ready to eat about six to eight weeks after the initial sowing.

Rosemary
(Rosmarinus officinalis)

One of the most appealing shrubs, rosemary has been used in both medicinal and culinary senses for centuries, and there are more legends attached to it than to any other herb. It loves the baking heat and dryness of the Mediterranean, but will grow to quite a good size in northern climates if given a warm, dry, sheltered place. It particularly likes the seaside – its name comes from the Latin for "dew of the sea". It has a great affinity with veal, pork and rabbit, and has always been a traditional accompaniment to lamb. Tuck sprigs into little slits in a roasting joint; under a rack or leg of lamb or veal before roasting; into the butter in which you are softening onions for a veal or rabbit stew; and drop a sprig into the oil in which you are frying potatoes. It also gives a wonderful flavour and aroma when burned on the barbecue coals. It can get into a bouquet garni, into aromatic jams and jellies, and if young leaves are finely chopped they can be added to sauces for fish and shellfish, and to scone and biscuit mixtures. Sprigs can be added to a jar of sugar to make rosemary sugar.

Rosemary is better fresh than dried, although it does dry successfully, and fresh rosemary had the added advantage of staying in one piece in the cooking – which is lucky as it is very disagreeable to eat a mouthful of the dried needle-like leaves. Rosemary can be used in pot-pourri.

Medicinal
Rosemary is antiseptic, and was one of the disinfectant strewing herbs of medieval times; it was also used in the posies carried by judges and by the monarch on Maundy Thursday, to protect them from contagion in public places. It is digestive, stimulant, and good for the heart (in tea or wine). It is high in calcium, and thus good for convalescents. A mouthwash for the gums and for bad breath can be made. Oil in which rosemary has been steeped is good when applied to aching muscles and joints; a sprig in the bathwater has the same effect. Rosemary's most renowned cosmetic benefit concerns the hair; an infusion can darken the colour of brown hair and stimulate its growth.

Cultivation
A perennial shrub, rosemary has needle-shaped, grey-green leaves and pale to deep blue flowers which appear from early spring to autumn. Seed is difficult to obtain and germination is slow, so the best method of propagation is from heel cuttings taken in early summer. It grows well in any well-drained soil, but prefers a sunny sheltered spot. Prune a larger bush regularly. Rosemary can also be grown in a container out of doors, but it should be brought indoors during the coldest part of the winter.

Sage
(Salvia officinalis)

There are many varieties of this herb, native to the northern Mediterranean, but the most commonly grown and used in cookery is *officinalis*. It is a powerful herb, harsh and dry but fragrant. The leaves are best known for their inclusion in stuffings (the famous sage and onion) for roast pork, goose, chicken and duck, and sage is an important ingredient – usefully lessening the impact of the fat – in pork pies and sausages. It may also be used – sparingly because of the strong flavour – sprinkled onto meat stews, chopped into green salads, cream cheese dips and spreads, and in fruit and wine cups. Partridge is sometimes cooked with sage, and eel and bacon wrapped in sage and grilled makes an interesting dish. In classic Italian cuisine, fresh sage is fried in the oil or butter in which veal escalopes or slices of calf's liver are to be cooked. Several English cheeses are flavoured with sage, notably Sage Derby. The leaves can be used fresh or dried; drying takes time because the leaves are more fleshy than those of other herbs. Dried sage leaves can be added to pot-pourri.

Medicinal
Sage was once believed to give wisdom and prolong life, and its generic name *salvia* comes from the Latin verb *salvere*, to save. It is a digestive – one reason why it is traditionally eaten with fattier foods like pork and goose – and generally tonic in effect; sage tea was an old remedy for colds, rheumatism and fevers. Sage was given to those suffering from respiratory disorders, and infusions are good for infections of the mouth, throat and teeth. Sage is a beauty herb as well, conditioning and darkening the hair. It is astringent, and a sage bath benefits the skin.

Cultivation
Sage is a hardy evergreen shrub which grows to a height of about 60cm (2ft); the leaves are generally a wrinkled grey-green and small violet-blue flowers appear in early summer. Seeds can be sown under glass in early spring, and transplanted in late spring, or directly into the garden in the mid to late part of the season. Sage likes a chalky, well-drained soil, in a sheltered site in full sun. It can also be propagated from heel cuttings in the autumn. It grows well in containers. The plant needs to be replaced every three or four years as it tends to become leggy. Gather the leaves for use or for drying in late spring just before the flowers appear, as the flavourful and healthful oils are then at their best.

Salad Burnet

(Sanguisorba minor)

S alad burnet – or burnet – notable for its grey-green leaves and cool cucumber flavour, was a familiar herb to our ancestors. An old rhyme goes: ". . . salad is neither good nor fair/If Pimpinella [burnet] is not there". It was planted in Tudor knot gardens, it was taken to the New World by the Pilgrim Fathers, and it was eaten by the exiled Napoleon in his daily haricot bean salad.

Mainly a salad herb as its name suggests, the young, very tender and tiny leaves can be sprinkled into the salad bowl with the lettuce – but sparingly, as many find them very bitter. They can also be added to raw vegetable salads. Finely chopped, the leaves can add flavour to cream cheeses for dips, sandwich spreads, herb butters and sauces (Ravigote and Chivry in particular). Burnet vinegar has an interesting tang when used in salad dressings. Salad burnet is a native of the Mediterranean, and is most popular in France and Italy, where it is still sold in bunches of mixed salad greens. The generic name, from the Greek *poterion*, a drinking cup, gives an indication of burnet's most common usage – as a flavouring and garnish, like borage, for white wine cups and cooling summer drinks. The leaves can be frozen or dried.

Medicinal

Burnet has proved most useful throughout the centuries as it is one of the few herbs that stay green all winter. It has always been considered a general tonic, whether eaten or taken as a tea, and was originally used to flavour wine, especially claret, which would enliven the mind, and "drive away melancholy". It is mildly diuretic, and has a cleansing effect on the liver and kidneys. Cosmetically, an infusion of burnet will strengthen and refine the facial skin or the body if used in the bath.

Cultivation

A hardy perennial herb, salad burnet grows to a height of about 30–40cm (12–15in), with oval toothed leaflets; flowers, globular heads of green turning to red, appear throughout the summer. Plant seed in a sunny position in good garden soil – it likes chalk best – during late spring or early autumn. Keep flower heads cut back to encourage growth of young leaves. If flowers are retained, the plant will seed itself successfully. It grows commonly in the wild, and can be grown in containers.

Summer Savory

(Satureja hortensis)

Savory is a herb that is little appreciated in British or American cookery, but is valued on the Continent – in France, Switzerland and Germany in particular – where it is known as the "bean-herb". There are two distinct varieties: the winter savory *(satureja montana)* is generally regarded as poorer in flavour. Aromatic and pleasantly bitter with a scent and flavour a little like thyme, summer savory was used by the Romans to flavour vinegar in much the same way as we use mint in mint sauce today: it could still be used thus for a flavourful vinegar in salad dressings. It must be used with discretion, though, as it can be overpowering. In France where it is called *sarriette*, it is used with thyme to flavour rabbit, and fresh sprigs are cooked with broad beans and peas. It can be sprinkled onto vegetable soups and meat broths, and used to give flavour to roast meats and sauces. In France, savory is occasionally used as a traditional covering for small local cheeses. It dries well, and can be used with other herbs in stuffings for turkey and veal.

Medicinal

Savory is traditionally associated with beans because, not only does it improve their flavour, but it has a strong digestive effect which counteracts the flatulence suffered by many after eating beans or pulses. It has also been thought variously to be strengthening and exhilarating, to relieve tired eyes, to preserve hearing, and to ease the swelling of bee or wasp stings. Dried savory can be used in pot-pourri.

Cultivation

Summer savory is a bushy hardy annual, growing to a height of about 30cm (12in). It has long, narrow, dark green leaves, and tiny pink-lilac flowers which appear from early to late summer. Sow seeds in a sunny position in any fertile, well-drained soil in mid spring, and thin when seedlings are large enough to handle. It can be grown successfully in a container or pot, and it will provide fresh leaves throughout the winter.

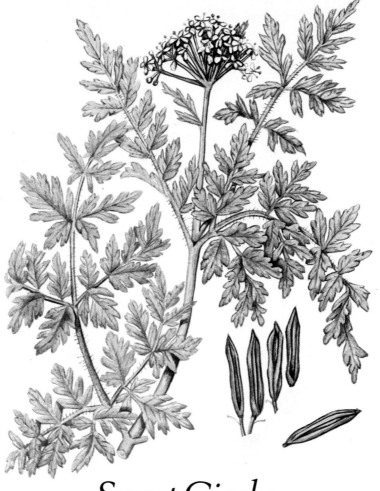

Sweet Cicely

(Myrrhis odorata)

A pretty old-fashioned herb which grows in profusion in herb gardens and in the wild. It is a member of the *umbelliferae* family, related to chervil, fennel, dill, and coriander. It is also known as anise chervil – *cerfeuil musque* in France – and myrrh, references to the smell of the plant. Both the leaves and the long green-black seeds can be used – the taste is somewhere between anise and liquorice, fragrant and sugary. And because of this, sweet cicely is also known as the "sugar-saver" herb: it reduces the acidity of tart fruit such as rhubarb, gooseberries, redcurrants, and plums, and thus helps to cut down on the quantity of sugar required. The roots of the plant were once boiled like parsnips, as were the stems; the leaves can be chopped into salads, into soups or stews, sauces and dressings, and are particularly good cooked with root vegetables or added to all sorts of cream and fruit desserts. The seeds too can be chopped for many of the same uses; they were once used in the making of polish to clean and perfume oak floors and furniture. Sweet cicely used to be one of the ingredients of Chartreuse, and it dries well.

Medicinal

Because of its reputation as a sugar-saver, sweet cicely is valuable for those who wish to cut down on sugar consumption – diabetics, slimmers and all those who are protecting their teeth and health in general. An older reputation concerns its use as a digestive; the boiled roots were given to the elderly in order to strengthen their digestion. The seeds can be chewed to counter indigestion, and a tea is restorative (it does not require sweetening).

Cultivation

Sweet cicely is an extremely decorative, slow-growing perennial. It can grow to about 1.2m (4ft) tall; it has fern-like leaves and tiny white flowers in clusters which appear in late spring and early summer. Sow seeds in early spring in moist soil in partial shade; and thin when seedlings are large enough to handle. The plant can be moved easily, and it seeds itself successfully, although a majority of the flower heads should be removed to allow the leaf flavour to develop. Sweet cicely is particularly valuable in that it can be picked throughout most of the year.

Sweet Woodruff

(Asperula odorata)

A small creeping woodland herb (it grows mainly among beeches), sweet woodruff has a ravishing hay-like perfume which becomes stronger and more intense when the herb is cut and partially dried. It is immensely popular on the Continent where it is traditionally used in "May drinks": the flowers appear for a brief period in late spring, when the plant and its aroma and flavour are at their best. In Germany, the *Maitrink* is made by infusing woodruff in Rhine wine; in the USA, it goes in a May wine punch. For a home-made version, steep the well-washed plants in a jug of white wine overnight in the refrigerator, add brandy and sugar or Benedictine, and serve with a garnish of the green leaves. Try other, less alcoholic summer drinks: place a few sprigs of partially dried woodruff in apple or other fruit juices.

Medicinal

Woodruff was once dried and placed in drawers and trunks to keep moths away; it was also a strewing herb. Its traditional use in wine cups or fruit punches is due to its reputation – similar to that of borage – as an exhilarating herb, relaxing and banishing depression. Woodruff tea or tisane has the same effect, and is also said to be good for headaches and migraines. A strong decoction has blood-cleansing properties, is good for the liver, and is said (paradoxically, considering its uplifting properties) to help induce long and sound sleep.

Cultivation

Sweet woodruff is a perennial, growing to a height of about 22–30cm (9–12in); it has whorls of pointed, mid-green leaves and cross-shaped fragrant flowers of a pure white which appear, obviously, in May (although sometimes in June too). In the wild, woodruff is found in woodland; in cultivation it is best used as ground cover under trees or large shrubs. Sow seeds in summer in light but moist soil, and thin in autumn. Propagate by division of roots in spring. The burr-like seeds will spread by means of sticking to fur or feather of passing creatures.

Tarragon
(Artemisia dracunculus)

French tarragon is one of the most valued culinary herbs. Like basil and dill, it has an addictive flavour – that is to say, those who have eaten it fresh can't very well get through the summer without it, since it is so delicious. French tarragon tastes sweetly of vanilla and aniseed, slightly sweet and bitter all at the same time, and quite unlike any other herb. It is particularly famed for its use with chicken, but it can be used in many other ways, harmonizing completely with all kinds of egg dishes, and lending its subtlety to savoury butters and creams. It is good in green and potato salads, and with cold salmon or trout; sprigs steeped in white wine vinegar are excellent in a French dressing as well as for the mayonnaise used for potato salad and to accompany cold fish. It is particularly effective in light buttery sauces for the milder vegetables like asparagus, and it flavours classic sauces like Béarnaise, Hollandaise and Mousseline. Chopped, it is one of the *fines herbes*. Dried tarragon takes on an uncharacteristic, hay-like flavour, but frozen tarragon is very good.

Russian tarragon (*artemisia dracunculoides*), unlike the true French herb, has a dull and disappointing flavour.

Medicinal
Tarragon is such an important culinary herb that it has not often been used for medicinal purposes. Like many other herbs, though, it helps the digestion; it was taken thus as a tisane by the maharajahs of India. Modern aromatherapists consider it effective in the treatment of menstrual problems such as amenorrhoea (cessation of menstruation) and PMT (pre-menstrual tension). It can also be used, finely chopped, as a seasoning for those who must avoid salt.

Cultivation
A hardy perennial, French tarragon can grow to a height of about 45–60cm (18–24in); it has linear, grey-green leaves, and tiny green-white globular flowers in late summer. These rarely open fully or produce viable seeds in temperate climates, and this is one way of telling the Russians from the French: if the plant *does* set seed, it is Russian. Sow seeds in the autumn or early spring in a sunny but sheltered position in light, very well-drained soil. Tarragon can also be propagated by taking cuttings of rooted shoots, or by replanting rhizomes. Encourage leaf growth by nipping out flowering stems as they appear, and replace plants every two or three seasons as the flavour of the leaves deteriorates. Tarragon can be grown in large pots, and brought indoors during the winter.

Thyme

(Thymus spp)

There are many varieties of thyme, but only a few are of use in the kitchen – principally garden or common thyme *(vulgaris)* and lemon thyme *(citriodorus)*. Thyme is one of the great culinary herbs, and is a classic constituent of a bouquet garni. Sun-loving, tiny-leafed but tough, it tastes and smells warm, earthy and flowery: it is clove-like and pungent, and should always be added to food with a certain amount of discretion. Use it in every kind of long-simmered and red-wine dish, with rabbit, veal and chicken in all their tomatoey forms, in jugged hare, in marinade and – instead of rosemary – with lamb. In Marseilles, thyme is sprinkled into everything including vinaigrettes, and over fish to be grilled on a wood fire. It gives pungency to pâtés, terrines and meatballs, and has an affinity with Mediterranean vegetables such as aubergines, courgettes and sweet peppers. It is also delicious with mushrooms. Commercially, thyme is used in soaps, antiseptic preparations, and in the liqueur Benedictine.

Lemon thyme is superb in stuffings for pork and veal – because of its strong lemon flavour, no lemon peel need be added – and can also be used in fruit salads, jellies and custards.

Home-dried thyme retains its flavour wonderfully, and is incomparably better than commercially dried or powdered thyme. To dry, hang in bunches in a warm place, then rub the leaves off and store in a jar.

Medicinal

Thyme contains thymol which is a powerful antiseptic – it was used as such in judges' and monarchs' posies to protect against contagious diseases. This property is still effective when thyme is used in made-up meat and fish dishes such as sausages. It makes a good mouthwash for bad breath, gum diseases and the inflammations associated with toothache. Tisanes calm and tranquillize, easing sleep, headaches and colds. Lemon thyme added to the bath relieves fatigue; thyme oil helps backache; and thyme in a herb pillow, in a pot-pourri, even growing in a pot, will act as a tonic, helping asthma and hayfever sufferers in particular.

Cultivation

Thyme grows wild as well as in cultivation; the flavour of wild thyme is usually milder. Common thyme is a small perennial bush of about 25cm (10in) high; the leaves are dark green, long and narrow (although golden-leaved varieties occur), and clusters of tubular mauve-pink flowers appear in early summer. Lemon thyme has slightly broader, lemon-scented leaves and minimally larger flowers. Sow seed outdoors in early spring in light, well-drained soil in a sunny position, and thin later. Propagate by root division or heel cuttings. Thyme is a good rock-garden plant as it spreads easily (indeed there is a creeping thyme which can be used in aromatic lawns), and it grows happily in containers.

OTHER HERBS, LEAVES AND FLOWERS

These are a selection of other herbs, both culinary, cosmetic and medicinal, without which the full spectrum of beneficial herbs could not be complete.

Bergamot
(Monarda didyma)

A perennial plant, red bergamot is also known as bee balm, and has vivid red flowers that smell and taste rather like mint. The leaves can be added to salads, wine or fruit drinks, and the flowers can be candied/crystallized. It is the major constituent of a relaxing and soporific tea, the one enjoyed by Americans after the Boston Tea Party, called Oswego. An oil can be used in the bathwater, and the leaves and flowers add fragrance to pot-pourri.

Chamomile or Camomile
(Anthemis nobilis)

A self-seeding and spreading plant with pretty, daisy-like flowers, chamomile is popularly used for aromatic lawns – there are chamomile lawns in the grounds of Buckingham Palace – and it smells faintly of apples when stepped on. A tea can relieve menstrual pains, stomach upsets and indigestion; this is especially good for the young (rabbits *or* children) as it is so mild: "Peter was not very well during the evening. His mother put him to bed, and made some camomile tea" (*Peter Rabbit*, Beatrix Potter). Small sprigs of chamomile can be added to salads and sauces; and infusions make a good herbal rinse for fair hair, and are also good for the skin and eyes.

Celery Leaves
(Apium graveolens)

Celery is a familiar garden vegetable, but the leaves are often discounted in a culinary sense. They can happily be used as a herb, however, as they contain much of the flavour of the plant, and will withstand long cooking (as indeed can the seeds, used as a spice). Use the leaves as a garnish and in salads, and in stuffings, stocks and stews. They are good medicinally for anyone on a salt-reduced diet as they add so much spicy flavour. Use celeriac leaves similarly.

Coltsfoot
(Tussilago farfara)

A perennial herb found commonly in the wild, coltsfoot's golden flowers appear in the early spring, before the leaves appear (in fact an old country name is Son-Before-Father because of this phenomenon). Coltsfoot is one of the oldest remedies for coughs, catarrh and chest complaints in general (its generic name comes from the Latin *tussil*, meaning cough), and the flowers and leaves were once dried and inhaled or smoked as a remedy for asthma and bronchitis. It is rich in vitamin C, so is a good internal cleanser taken as a tea in spring. Infusions are good for freshening the skin, and for benefitting spots and thread capillary problems; they are also good for puffy eyes. A wine is made from coltsfoot flowers, and the leaves can also be eaten.

Comfrey
(Symphytum officinale)

A large, coarse and furry-leaved plant with blue or creamy-white flowers, comfrey's main significance is in herbal medicine and cosmetics, although the leaves can be eaten, either cooked as a vegetable or made into fritters. Comfrey can cure coughs and bronchial ailments, and can be used as a wound-healing poultice – it contains allantoin which is said to stimulate the cells and encourage fast healing. For this reason it is one of the most popular herbs to use for healing and softening a sensitive or spotty skin, when both leaves and root can be used. Comfrey is also known variously as boneset and knit-bone, local names from its reputed use as a mash that would set hard like plaster over a broken bone. It grows commonly in the wild.

Dandelion
(Taraxacum officinale)

A wild perennial herb, generally considered a garden pest, young dandelion leaves (which can be found and picked at any time of the year) are good and peppery in salads or as a green vegetable. (Young plants can be blanched while growing, rather like chicory, to lessen their bitterness.) The leaves are highly nutritious, and their chief attribute is their use as a diuretic (echoed graphically in a French name for them, *pissenlit*): they also have blood-cleansing and digestive properties. Eating the leaves helps clear spots; a tea of fresh or dried leaves aids the liver and gall bladder functions; and dandelion juice is said to be useful in getting rid of warts or verrucas. The roots are dried, roasted and ground for a caffeine-free coffee substitute; the Japanese eat them boiled as a vegetable. The flowers can be made into a wine.

Elder
(Sambucus nigra)

A hardy deciduous shrub which grows in hedgerows and gardens, elder is used in cooking, medicine and cosmetics. The flowers are used in making wine, champagne or lemonade, and can be battered and deep-fried as fritters or used in pancake mixtures; infused, they make a good skin cleanser, a skin tonic or lotion particularly good for getting rid of freckles, and a soothing tea which is diuretic and will relieve colds. The berries make a wine too, and can be used in healthy jams and jellies; a berry syrup or juice relieves coughs and colds in winter.

Eyebright
(Euphrasia officinalis)

A small delicate annual, eyebright, as its name suggests, is very effective for the eyes. An infusion can relieve tired or inflamed eyes; a tea is tonic, good for digestion and helps hayfever; and a cosmetic skin lotion is cleansing and soothing.

Feverfew
(Tanacetum parthenium)

A little-known herb which has come to prominence very recently because of its success in treating migraine. Hospital research trials have suggested that eating four leaves a day (in a sandwich perhaps) can control incidence and severity of attacks. The leaves when chewed can also act as a mild laxative, and when rubbed on a sting relieve the pain.

Garlic
(Allium sativum)

A perennial bulb, garlic's main fame lies in its multifarious uses in the kitchen – crushed in stews, whole cloves baked with roasts, in garlicky sauces like aïoli and indeed in a soup. It was once highly regarded as a medicinal herb, for a clove a day is thought to have kept the slaves building the Pyramids healthy and active. It is strongly antiseptic like other members of the onion family: dressings of garlic were used during the world wars when other remedies were not available. If eaten regularly, garlic can prevent bronchitis and colds and high blood pressure. It is a good source of iodine. Garlic vinegar makes a particularly good salad dressing.

Geranium
(Pelargonium graveolens)

The scented leaves of various pelargoniums – their proper name – can be used in the kitchen: there are apple, rose, coconut, nutmeg, mint, orange and lemon scented varieties. The leaves of the rose geranium give a delicate rose flavour to some jellies and custards, to a cake if baked at the bottom of the pan, and to sherbets/sorbets or granitas if infused for about half an hour in a thin sugar syrup. Chopped rose geranium leaves can be added to soft fruit salads just before serving, and they can be left in a can of sugar for about a week, and the resultant scented sugar is delicious sprinkled over soft fruit, or used in baking. The leaves can be dried for a herbal tea or for pot-pourri, and the flowers can be candied/crystallized.

Hyssop
(Hyssopus officinalis)

A hardy evergreen perennial, hyssop can be grown in garden or pot. It is an ancient herb, once used in the preservation of meat; it is one of the flavourings of the liqueur Chartreuse. A few leaves – they have a bitter, minty flavour – can be used in salads, or they aid the digestion when cooked in lamb or rabbit stew; the flavour also goes well with stewed fruit and fruit pies. A tea is beneficial, helping clear the mucus of catarrh and colds; it is also effective for hayfever sufferers.

Lady's Mantle
(Alchemilla vulgaris)

A hardy perennial plant, lady's mantle was once known as the alchemists' herb, having a long and excellent reputation for healing. Its pale green flowers appear from May to September, but it is its leaves that are considered to be very effective in curing and aiding all women's complaints. A tea helps the internal organs, the menstrual cycle, is good during pregnancy and for those over the age of forty. Cosmetically, it is astringent, can be used to get rid of freckles, and is good for inflammations and acne.

Lavender
(Lavandula spica)

A small perennial shrub, lavender is usually thought of as a fragrant garden plant only, but it can be used in cooking. It has a sweet and musky perfume, and the spikes and leaves can be used in much the same way as rosemary (with a little more discretion perhaps). It can be used in a sweet herb mix – it is often included in *Herbes de Provence*, for instance – and it makes good herbal oils and vinegars. Lavendar oil can relieve burns, pain and stiffness; an infusion is an antidote for tension headaches and giddiness; and a compress of lavender vinegar held over the forehead can help headaches. Vital in pot-pourris, lavender can also be used in bags or cushions to help sleep and keep moths away, being particularly good for asthmatics.

Lemon Verbena
(Lippia citriodora)

A sweet-scented perennial shrub, lemon verbena can be grown in the herb garden or in a pot. Its lemon-flavoured leaves can be used – sparingly though – in fruit salads, punches and refreshing drinks, and they can also flavour custards, jams and sauces for fish. A tea has a mild sedative effect, and is good as a mouthwash for the gums (particularly so when mixed with a little mint). Dried leaves add fragrance to pot-pourri.

Lime
(Tillia spp)

The flowers of the deciduous lime tree (there are several varieties) can be collected, dried and made into linden tea (*tilleul* in France), which is famous for its delicious taste and soothing effect; it can reduce fevers, and is digestive and sedative. Infusions of lime flowers are good for the skin and hair. The leaves are sappy (this sap was once used to make sugar), and can reputedly be eaten as a sandwich filling.

Marigold
(Calendula officinalis)

A bright yellow-orange cottage-garden flower, marigolds can be used in cookery, medicine and cosmetics. The flowers make an economic alternative to saffron, and add colour to rice and cheese dishes and to puddings; they were the original colouring agent for cheese and butter. A petal tea – which helps the body utilize vitamin A – is good for the stomach and the complexion; a marigold oil is good for the skin (especially a sunburned one); marigold infusions can be added to the bathwater, to face packs, skin tonics and used as hair rinses; and a lotion is effective for cuts, bruises and spots.

Nasturtium

(Tropaeolum majus)
Almost every part of this pretty garden flower has a place in the kitchen, and its prime importance is that it is antibiotic and high in vitamin C and iron (thought to be highest in the leaves just before the plant flowers in July). Both the flowers and young leaves can be used in salads – they are rather like watercress in flavour, even hotter occasionally – and the buds and seeds can be pickled to make "capers". The leaves can be dried for a tea, and the flowers can be used too for a face steaming infusion. The flowers can also be candied/crystallized and used in pot-pourri.

Nettle

(Urtica dioica)
Like dandelions, nettles are considered a pest in the garden, and indeed can be unpleasant because of the stinging leaves, the hairs on which contain formic acid. (If for no other reason, nettles should always be allowed a little space in the garden, as many butterflies lay their eggs on them.) However, the young shoots and leaves may be cooked and eaten as a vegetable like spinach, and they are similarly rich in vitamins and iron, so are good for the skin, taken both externally and internally. A medicinal tea can be made from fresh or dried leaves. Nettles can also be made into a beer. A prime cosmetic function is as a hair tonic which is thought to prevent dandruff. They have "drawing out" properties and thus are good in an infusion for tired and aching feet.

Rose

(Rosaceae spp)
Both wild and cultivated roses can be used in cookery, in cosmetics and medicines. The petals once used to be made into rose syrup, rose candy and rose vinegar (the latter is still good for a delicate salad dressing); nowadays rose water is used lavishly by Middle Eastern cooks, and rose petals can be used in wine and jam and candied/crystallized for cake decorations. If dried carefully, petals and buds can be used in pot-pourri. Rose hips, particularly those of wild roses, are a rich source of vitamin C – a million birds can't be wrong – and purées, wine, jelly, soup, syrup and tea can be made from them. Rose water, bought or home-made, is a good skin tonic.

Rue

(Ruta graveolens)
A semi-evergreen shrub, rue is rarely used in cooking, as it is so bitter, but a couple of leaves can sharpen a salad or flavour a rich stew. Rue stems are steeped in the Sardinian spirit, *grappa con ruta*, where it is reputed to act digestively. Medicinally, it is antiseptic and was used as a strewing herb; it is also very effective against insects. A rue tea can be drunk to counteract dizziness and help menstrual disorders, and it can be applied to the eyes as a soothing lotion.

Sorrel

(Rumex acetosa)
A salad leaf which is used frequently in French cookery for its wonderfully acid taste: it makes a superb soup and sauces. It can be used in salads, cooked with spinach as a vegetable, in omelettes and soufflés – but in small amounts only, as it contains oxalic acid, undesirable in excess. It is diuretic, good for the kidneys and contains iron, like spinach, so is good for the blood.

Tansy

(Tanecetum vulgare)
A hardy perennial, this old-fashioned and once highly valued medicinal herb grows wild almost anywhere. Although bitter, its young leaves can be used very sparingly with egg and cheese dishes and puddings. It repels insects, and was thought to promote fertility. Cosmetically, it is slightly astringent when used in cleansers and lotions. It can be used as a spicy addition to pot-pourri.

Valerian

(Valeriana officinalis)
A hardy perennial, valerian grows in the wild, but is also quite happy in containers. (It is not the same valerian as that grown in gardens as a decorative plant.) Its name comes from the Latin *valere*, to be well, and it has long been considered a healing, medicinal herb. It is primarily thought of as *the* sedative herb; a decoction of the grated roots taken at bedtime will promote sound sleep (but it should not be too strong or taken too frequently) – and leaves in the bathwater will have the same effect. It is also useful as a tea to cure headaches, help asthma, and normalize the menstrual cycle. An ointment of the leaves or roots is good for skin complaints.

Violet

(Viola odorata)
A perennial garden flower (which also grows in the wild), violets were once used much more frequently in cookery. Nowadays the flowers can be candied/crystallized for decorating cakes or puddings, and fresh, they can add colour to salads. A tea can be made from the leaves, and infusions of the flowers are good for the skin.

Yarrow

(Achillea millefolium)
A hardy perennial, yarrow grows commonly in hedgerows, and was once a highly valued medicinal plant, as it has strong antiseptic properties, and could staunch wounds. Leaves can be added to salads, or eaten as a sandwich filling, but they are bitter and should not be taken in excess. Infusions of flowers are particularly good for greasy skin and hair, and a tea helps the stomach, colds, menstrual cramps and fevers.

COOKING WITH HERBS

The simplest and most natural way of using the goodness of herbs is to add them to food. Not only do they immeasurably improve the flavours of foods, but they can also contribute enormously to the value of the daily diet. The sprig of parsley with its high content of vitamin C immediately springs to mind, but many of the other properties of herbs are as important, particularly as regards digestion. Even before any food is actually eaten, the aroma of a herb is useful, for the sense of smell is a major constituent of the whole digestive process. Whether the herb is chopped up in a salad or a sprig is cooked gently in a casserole, its essential oils will be released and be detected by the nose: this starts the flow of saliva which is, literally, the beginning of digestion.

Herbs can also have value in that they can be used instead of seasonings – particularly useful for those on salt-reduced and other special diets. Lovage, thyme and marjoram add flavour and harmony to unsalted foods, and watercress, savory, basil and nasturtium leaves can be used for a certain spiciness. In fact, one of the top chefs in Britain has recently created particular mixtures of selected herbs which can season all sorts of foods, thereby reducing the need for salt and other seasonings by up to 50 per cent. Herbs can also be used effectively by those on slimming diets. Sweet cicely – the sugar-saver herb – helps to cut down on the amount of sugar used in sweet dishes. Angelica and lemon balm have slight sweetening powers too, while fennel, parsley and rose hips, although working in a different way, also have a place in a healthy reducing diet.

The traditional ways of using the individual herbs are defined elsewhere (on the herb identification pages, 31 to 61), and they are exemplified in many of the recipes on the following pages. These, however, can also be jumping-off points for your own experimentation: many combinations are possible, and most recipes can be adapted to suit what you have in the refrigerator or to take advantage of what is growing most profusely and successfully in your herb garden. No adventurous or imaginative cook should ever be too constricted by culinary convention. Use herbs lavishly or discreetly, depending on their strength and your taste – and do remember that dried herbs are more powerful than fresh; if a recipe states three tablespoons of fresh herbs, use one tablespoon only of dried.

HERB BASICS, STOCKS, SAUCES AND DRESSINGS

A bouquet garni is one of the most practical – and easy – ways of incorporating the flavour and goodness of herbs into the diet; it is vital in stocks which will be used as the basis of a soup or sauce. *Fines herbes,* too, are an almost magical way of adding interest, flavour and colour to a great many simple dishes, as well as to a number of sauces and dressings in this section.

Many of the classic sauces and salad dressings can also be enhanced by the use of herbs: add them to simple white flour sauces, to Béarnaise, to butter sauces, to mayonnaise, and to oil and vinegar dressings. Some traditional dishes in Britain rely upon a tangy herb sauce – roast beef with its horseradish sauce, lamb with its mint sauce. And where would the classic tomato sauce be without the sweet pungency of basil?

BOUQUET GARNI

The classic bouquet garni is composed of a few sprigs of parsley, a sprig of thyme and a bay leaf, but other herbs may be added or substituted – rosemary, marjoram, celery or celeriac leaves, or fennel sprigs for instance. Select the herbs to go with the dish you are cooking, and never use too many at one time or they will lose their individuality, cancelling each other out. Fresh herbs can simply be tied together, or tied up inside a celery stalk or outer leaf of a split leek; dried herbs can be wrapped in cheesecloth/muslin to make a little bag. The bouquet garni is added to the stock, soup, stew or casserole, and it is discarded when the dish is cooked; it can be suspended on string from a pot or casserole handle so that it is easy to remove.

FINES HERBES

This is usually a mixture of the more tender herbs such as chervil, parsley, chives and, occasionally, tarragon. They are all chopped very fine, and can flavour a multitude of dishes from delicately cooked eggs – try *fines herbes* in an omelette, in scrambled eggs, and with baked eggs – to plain cooked fish such as sole or plaice with a cream and white wine sauce. They are delicious too in a simple butter sauce (see page 65), with a squeeze of lemon, to accompany grilled or roast chicken, veal escalopes, or more delicate vegetables like asparagus. *Fines herbes* can go into tartare and Béarnaise sauces instead of or as well as the chives or tarragon, and they add colour and flavour to a mayonnaise to accompany shellfish and eggs.

BROWN STOCK

Brown stock is made in the same way as bone stock, below, except that the bones are browned in dripping in a roasting pan before being put into the stock pot.

WHITE STOCK

Use veal knuckle bones and ½ lb/225 g stewing veal instead of the beef, below.

BONE STOCK

Lovage could be added to the bouquet garni to contribute its unique, meaty flavour.

Makes about 6 cups/1.5 litres

4 lb/2 kg beef marrowbones, sawn into short lengths
12 cups/3 litres water
1 lb/450g beef shin
¼ lb/125g bacon trimmings
2 onions, peeled and sliced
2 carrots, trimmed and sliced
1 celery stalk, sliced mushroom trimmings and stalks
2 leeks, trimmed and cut in half
1 bouquet garni (see above)

1 Wrap the bones in cheesecloth/muslin to prevent the loss of the marrow and put them into a large pot. Pour on the water and bring it slowly to the boil. As it begins to boil, skim off the foam.
2 Add the remaining ingredients, half cover the pot, and simmer gently for 1 hour.
3 Remove the vegetables – all their flavour will have been extracted – and continue simmering for a further 2 hours. Do not let the stock boil quickly or it will become cloudy.
4 Strain the stock into a bowl through a colander lined with wet cheesecloth/muslin. When cool, cover the bowl and put it in the refrigerator. Keep for no longer than 1 week.

VEGETABLE STOCK

Vegetable stock, being so delicately flavoured, is ideal for many herb soups.

Makes about 6 cups/1.5 litres

2 tbs/25g butter
1 lb/450g carrots, cut into large pieces
1 lb/450g onions, peeled and cut into large pieces
6 celery stalks, cut into large pieces
½ lb/225g turnips, peeled and cut into large pieces
1 leek, trimmed and sliced
1 bouquet garni (see above)
6 peppercorns
2 tsp salt
12 cups/3 litres hot water

1 Melt the butter in a large pan or casserole. Add the vegetables and cook them over low heat, stirring frequently, until they are brown.
2 Add the remaining ingredients and the water and bring it to the boil. Partially cover the pan and simmer for 3 hours. The liquid should have reduced to about one-third of the original volume.
3 Pour the stock into a bowl through a colander lined with wet cheesecloth/muslin. Cool the stock, then store it in the refrigerator – for no longer than a week – until needed.

FISH STOCK

Fish stock is used to make sauces that are required to coat a finished fish dish. If the fish seller is filleting fish for you, be sure to ask for the heads and bones – and some extra ones if you feel you will need them.

Makes about 5 cups/1 litre

> 1 lb/450g fish bones from sole,
> flounder/plaice, turbot
> or whiting
> 1 onion, sliced
> 1 oz/25g parsley or parsley stalks
> (which contain the
> most flavour)
> 2 tbs/25g butter
> strips of lemon peel
> $\frac{1}{4}$ cup/65 ml white wine
> 6 peppercorns
> 1 tsp salt
> 5 cups/1 litre cold water

1 Break the bones into pieces and put them into a pan with all the other ingredients.
2 Partly cover the pan and simmer the stock for 20 minutes.
3 Pour the stock through a sieve into a bowl, cool and then keep in the refrigerator for no longer than a couple of days.

CHICKEN OR GAME BIRD STOCK

For stock made with only the carcass, proceed as for bone stock, but cook for only 1 hour. The best chicken stock, however, is made from a jointed boiling fowl, which should simmer for 3 hours. A good chicken stock can also be made from chicken wings, necks and backs.

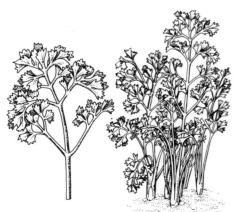

Parsley

COURT BOUILLON

This is basically a seasoned acidic liquid in which such large whole fish as salmon, turbot and trout are cooked. Fennel sprigs could replace the thyme.

Makes about 6 cups/1.5 litres

> $\frac{2}{3}$ cup/150 ml white wine
> $8\frac{3}{4}$ cups/2 litres water
> 2 onions, peeled
> $\frac{1}{2}$ lb/225g carrots, sliced
> 1 bay leaf
> 1 large thyme sprig
> $1\frac{1}{4}$ oz/30g salt
> $\frac{2}{3}$ cup/150 ml tarragon vinegar
> 1 oz/25g parsley, with stalks
> 12 peppercorns

1 Put all the ingredients into a saucepan and bring to just under boiling point.
2 Simmer gently for 1 hour.
3 Strain, cool and refrigerate until needed.

MINT SAUCE

Makes about $\frac{1}{4}$ cup/65 ml

> 1 large handful of
> mint leaves
> 2 tbs boiling water
> 3 tbs wine or mint vinegar
> salt
> 1 tbs superfine/caster sugar

1 Wash and dry the mint leaves.
2 Chop them very finely or cut them up with scissors in a cup, and put them in a bowl.
3 Pour on the boiling water to set the colour.
4 Stir in the vinegar, salt and sugar.

HORSERADISH SAUCE

Serve this sauce with roast beef.

Makes $\frac{2}{3}$ cup/150 ml

> 3 tbs grated horseradish
> $\frac{2}{3}$ cup/150 ml unflavoured/natural
> yogurt or heavy/
> double cream
> salt
> freshly ground
> black pepper

1 Put the horseradish into a mixing bowl, and stir in the yogurt or cream, salt and pepper.
2 Set aside for at least 1 hour before serving to allow the flavours to develop.

BÉCHAMEL SAUCE

Chopped herbs can be added to this sauce to give colour and flavour – parsley is a favourite – but you can also add the flavour of other herbs (without the colour) by simmering the leaves in the milk first. Try lemon verbena, lemon balm, chervil, sage, lovage, garlic or savory. Use about 8 leaves, and simmer in the milk for 10–15 minutes before straining out the leaves.

Makes about $1\frac{1}{4}$ cups/300 ml

> $1\frac{1}{4}$ cups/300 ml milk
> 1 mace blade
> 1 bouquet garni (see page
> 63)
> 4 white peppercorns
> 1 shallot, peeled and sliced
> $1\frac{1}{2}$ tbs/20g butter
> $1\frac{1}{2}$ tbs/20g flour
> salt

1 Put the milk, mace, bouquet garni, peppercorns and shallot in a small saucepan and place it over a very low heat for 5–10 minutes to infuse. Strain the milk and set aside.
2 Melt the butter in a small pan. Stir in the flour and remove the pan from the heat.
3 Gradually stir in the strained milk, and beat well to prevent lumps forming.
4 Stirring constantly, cook over moderate heat until the sauce boils. Season to taste.

BÉARNAISE SAUCE

Tarragon is the classic flavouring for Béarnaise, but other herbs, notably chervil, can also be used.

Makes $\frac{3}{4}$ cup/175 ml

> 4 tbs white wine
> 2 tbs white wine (or tarragon)
> vinegar
> 1 bay leaf
> 1 mace blade
> 1 shallot
> 4 peppercorns
> 2 egg yolks
> $\frac{1}{2}$ cup/125g softened butter
> salt
> 2 tsp finely chopped tarragon
> freshly ground
> black pepper

1 Put the wine, vinegar, bay leaf, mace, shallot and peppercorns into a small pan. Bring the liquid to the boil and cook

until it is reduced to 2 tablespoons. Strain the liquid and set aside.

2 In the top of a double saucepan or in a small bowl over a pan of water, mix the egg yolks with 1 teaspoon of the butter and a pinch of salt. Pour the strained vinegar onto the egg mixture and stir to mix.

3 Place the double saucepan or bowl and pan over the heat – the water must be hot but not boiling – and whisk the egg mixture until it has thickened.

4 Gradually add the rest of the butter, $\frac{1}{2}$ teaspoon at a time, stirring constantly, until the sauce is like whipped cream.

5 Add the tarragon and seasoning to taste.

GREEN SAUCE

Makes $1\frac{1}{4}$ cups/300 ml

10 watercress sprigs
4 parsley sprigs
4 tarragon sprigs
10 spinach leaves
salt
$1\frac{1}{4}$ cups/300 ml mayonnaise (see below)

1 In a small saucepan boil the watercress, parsley, tarragon and spinach for 3 minutes in a little salted water.

2 Drain the herbs and spinach, reserving 1 tablespoon of the liquor.

3 Rub the greens through a sieve.

4 Mix the purée into the mayonnaise with the reserved tablespoon of cooking liquor.

SORREL SAUCE

This sauce is particularly good served with hot baked or poached fish like trout. A spoonful of well reduced fish poaching liquid can also be added to the sauce.

Makes about $\frac{2}{3}$ cup/50 ml

4 oz/100g sorrel leaves
2 tbs/25g butter
$\frac{2}{3}$ cup/150 ml cultured sour cream
a pinch each of sugar,
salt and freshly
ground pepper

1 Wash and dry the sorrel leaves, chop finely, and sweat in the melted butter over a low heat for 5 minutes.

2 Stir in the cultured sour cream. Heat gently and season to taste.

TARRAGON, DILL OR FENNEL SAUCE

Prepare as for Sorrel Sauce, but use a smaller quantity of herbs. A lighter and less fattening version of these sauces can be made by replacing half of the cultured sour cream with thick Greek yogurt or a low-fat soft or cream cheese.

HERB BUTTER SAUCES

Melt all the ingredients for hot sauces slowly together over a low heat. Try making fines herbes (see page 63), fennel, chervil, tarragon, savory, garlic and parsley butter sauces in the same way as chive.

Chive Butter
4 tbs/50g butter
2 tbs finely chopped chives
a few drops of lemon juice
freshly ground black pepper and mace to taste

Lemon Herb Butter
4 tbs/50g butter
1 small lemon, rind and juice
1 tbs finely chopped mixed herbs (tarragon, parsley, etc)
a pinch each of sugar, salt and freshly ground black pepper

Orange Mint Butter
4 tbs/50g butter
1 small orange, rind and juice
1 tbs finely chopped fresh mint
a pinch of freshly ground black pepper and mace

COLD HERB BUTTERS

For small slices to use as garnishes on grilled fish or steaks, work flavourings and herbs as above into softened butter. Roll into a log shape and wrap in foil or wax/greaseproof paper. Chill or freeze until firm (do *not* freeze garlic butter). Slice and serve cold on top of hot food.

MAYONNAISE

For a herb mayonnaise, add about 1–2 tablespoons finely chopped herb of your choice – or fines herbes (see page 63) – to the basic recipe. For a garlic mayonnaise (or aïoli), first mix the egg yolks with about 4–5 peeled and crushed garlic cloves.

Makes about $1\frac{1}{4}$ cups/300 ml

2 egg yolks
$\frac{1}{2}$ tsp salt
$\frac{1}{2}$ tsp French mustard
$1\frac{1}{4}$ cups/300 ml olive oil
2 tsp wine or herb vinegar, or the juice of $\frac{1}{2}$ lemon

1 Using a wooden spoon, mix the egg yolks well with the salt and mustard in a mixing bowl.

2 With the oil in a measuring jug, begin pouring it onto the yolks, drop by drop, beating all the time. Continue pouring and beating, adding the oil more quickly as the mayonnaise thickens. When all the oil has been incorporated the sauce will be very thick and glossy.

3 Fold in the vinegar or lemon juice very carefully.

4 To make mayonnaise in a liquidizer, first blend the egg yolks and salt together, then slowly, drop by drop, begin to add the oil through the hole in the lid, gradually pouring in a steady stream. Finally add vinegar or lemon juice and mustard.

BASIC HERB VINAIGRETTE DRESSING

Makes about $\frac{1}{2}$ cup/125 ml

2 tbs wine or herb vinegar, or lemon juice
5–6 tbs corn, olive or sunflower oil
a pinch of dried mustard powder
salt
freshly ground black pepper
1 tbs finely chopped fresh herb (parsley, chervil, mint, tarragon, oregano or basil)

1 Put the vinegar or lemon juice into a small bowl with the oil.

2 Add the mustard powder, and salt and pepper to taste.

3 Whisk until well blended, and the ingredients have formed a smooth emulsion.

4 Mix the herbs and stand for a while before using so that the flavours blend. Mix again before use.

SOUPS AND STARTERS

Soups, whether hot or cold, make an appetizing and delicious start to a meal, and they also provide one of the best opportunities for using the flavour of herbs. Some herbs, like parsley, nettles, garlic or lovage can form the actual basis of a soup, and thyme or rosemary, for instance, can contribute their flavour to another major ingredient. Many other herbs – the ones which might dominate or which would lose their flavour and goodness if cooked for a long time – can be sprinkled onto the surface of a soup at the last moment. Their vivid green colour gives visual appeal, and contributes a fresh flavour.

A herb-flavoured stock can be used as the basis of a light soup or "consommé", and it's easily made by infusion. Heat a well flavoured stock until boiling, then move from the heat. Add several tablespoons of the chopped herb – dill, tarragon or chervil, for instance – and leave to infuse for about 30 minutes. Strain and use as a clear soup – with some finely chopped vegetables lightly cooked in it, perhaps – and sprinkled at the last moment with a little of the same chopped herb.

Starters other than soups can encompass a vast variety of ingredients – and herbs can make their appearance happily here, whether as a vital ingredient or the finishing garnishing touch (which should always be eaten: never waste all that goodness on visual delights alone). Pâtés benefit enormously from the inclusion of herbs, particularly the "meat" herbs like marjoram and thyme; and they could not look so splendid without their crowning garnish of bay leaves. Tarts, flans and quiches make a good starter too: each will cut into eight wedges (or four for a main course).

GARLIC SOUP

Serves 4

8 large garlic cloves, peeled
½ lb/225g potatoes, peeled and diced
1 bay leaf
1 thyme sprig
1 sage leaf
1 basil leaf
salt
freshly ground black pepper

1 Put the peeled garlic cloves and the potato dice into a saucepan.
2 Pour in 4 cups/900 ml water, and add the remaining ingredients.
3 Bring to the boil, cover the pan, reduce the heat and simmer for 30 minutes.
4 Pour the soup into a liquidizer and blend it well. Return the soup to the pan, reheat and adjust the seasoning. Serve hot.

TOMATO AND ROSEMARY SOUP

Serves 4

1 lb/450g ripe tomatoes
1 large onion, chopped
¾ lb/350g potatoes, peeled and diced
½ lemon, rind and juice
2½ cups/625 ml chicken or vegetable stock (see page 64)
4 rosemary sprigs
salt
freshly ground black pepper

1 Put the tomatoes into a saucepan, and add the onion, potatoes, and lemon rind and juice.
2 Pour in the well seasoned stock with the rosemary sprigs, plus salt and pepper to taste.
3 Cover the pan and simmer the soup gently for 30 minutes, or until the tomatoes are very soft.
4 Sieve the soup or liquidize it and then sieve to remove the tomato seeds and skins.
5 Return the puréed soup to the pan, adjust the seasoning to taste and reheat.

BEAN SOUP

Serves 4

½ lb/225g dried butter beans
1 onion, peeled and chopped
2 celery stalks, chopped
1 large carrot, scrubbed and sliced
½ lemon, rind and juice
1 bay leaf
2½–3½ cups/ 625–900 ml beef stock (see page 63)
2 tbs finely chopped borage or savory leaves (optional)
salt
freshly ground black pepper

1 Soak the beans in 2½ cups/625 ml cold water overnight – or soak them in the same quantity of boiling water for 2 hours.

2 Drain the beans, reserving the water, and put in a large saucepan along with the onion, celery, carrot, lemon rind and juice, and the bay leaf.

3 Add enough stock to the soaking liquid to make it up to 5 cups/1 litre, then pour over the beans and vegetables.

4 Cover the pan and bring to the boil. Reduce the heat and simmer gently for 2 hours, or until the beans are tender.

5 Liquidize or sieve the soup, and return to the cleaned pan.

6 Add the chopped herb leaves if used, and salt and pepper to taste. Reheat, and add a little more stock if necessary.

SUMMER SOUP

This soup comes from a farm near the great house of Luton Hoo. It was written out in an early 19th-century collection of recipes which came from a cook at the great house. The soup depends on all the vegetables and herbs being fresh from the garden. It should be served chilled, with very hot triangles of cheese pastry.

Serves 4

1 lettuce, trimmed, well washed and cut into ½in/1cm strips
¼ lb/125g spinach, chopped
1 cucumber, peeled and cut into ½in/1 cm cubes
8 shallots or 2 medium onions or 12 scallions/ spring onions, chopped
½ lb/225g potatoes, peeled and cut into ½in/1cm cubes
5 cups/1 litre chicken stock (see page 64)
12 parsley sprigs
2 bay leaves
6 thyme sprigs
3 lemon thyme sprigs
½ tsp salt
½ tsp freshly ground black pepper
1¼ cups/300 ml heavy/double cream
1 tbs finely chopped mint and parsley mixed
Pastry triangles
½ lb/225g short/shortcrust pastry
⅔ cup/60g grated Cheddar cheese
¼ tsp cayenne pepper
1 egg yolk, beaten

1 Put all the vegetables into a saucepan with the stock. Tie the herbs in a bunch and add to the pan with the salt and pepper. Bring to the boil and simmer, covered, for 30 minutes.

2 Remove the herbs and allow the soup to get cold; when cold stir in all but a tablespoon of the cream. Put the soup in the refrigerator to chill for at least 1 hour before serving.

3 Meanwhile, roll out the pastry, sprinkle with the cheese, and the cayenne pepper, fold over and roll out to about ¼in/6mm thick. Cut the pastry into neat triangles, brush over with the beaten egg yolk, and bake at 400°F/200°C, Gas Mark 6 for 10 minutes.

4 Ladle the chilled soup into four bowls. Put a teaspoon of cream on top of each and sprinkle with the chopped mint and parsley. Serve with the hot pastry triangles.

LOVAGE SOUP

A parsley soup could be made in the same way. For a chervil soup, omit the milk, add the juice of ½ lemon, and thicken at the end with an egg yolk. Garnish with whipped cream.

Serves 6

2 onions, peeled and sliced
2 tbs/25g butter
3 tbs finely chopped fresh lovage
1 oz/25g all-purpose/plain flour
4 large potatoes, peeled and sliced
5 cups/1 litre good chicken stock (see page 64)
salt
freshly ground black pepper
1¼ cups/300 ml milk
2 tbs finely chopped fresh parsley

1 Sauté the onions in the butter for about 5 minutes until softened, then add the lovage and the flour.

2 Cook for a few minutes longer over a gentle heat, stirring, and then add the potato slices, stock, salt and pepper.

3 Cover and simmer for about 25 minutes, or until the potato is soft.

4 Add the milk then purée the soup in the blender, or push through a sieve.

5 Return to a clean pan, taste for seasoning, and reheat gently. Serve hot, sprinkled with parsley.

MUSSEL SOUP WITH THYME

The addition of fresh thyme at the very last moment gives this richly flavoured soup a wonderful fragrance.

Serves 4

9 cups/2 litres mussels (in shells)
2½ cups/625 ml dry white wine
5 cups/1 litre fish stock (see page 64)
4 tbs olive oil
5oz/150g carrots, peeled and finely chopped
1 medium onion, peeled and finely chopped
2 garlic cloves, peeled and finely chopped
2 tbs tomato paste/purée
a pinch of saffron
1 small bouquet garni (see page 63)
1¼ cups/300 ml heavy/double or whipping cream
salt
freshly ground black pepper
1 fresh thyme sprig

1 Sort through the mussels, scrub them well, remove their beards and throw out any that are damaged or open. Wash in several changes of fresh water to clean them.

2 Put the mussels into a large saucepan with the dry white wine and fish stock and cook briskly with the lid on until the shells are just open. Drain off the juice and keep separate. Discard any mussels that have not opened.

3 Warm the olive oil and sweat the finely chopped carrots, onion and garlic for about 10 minutes over a low heat (with the lid on). Add the juice from the mussels, then the tomato paste/purée, saffron and bouquet garni.

4 Cover and cook gently for 30–40 minutes. Meanwhile remove the mussels from their shells and keep hot.

5 When the carrots and other vegetables are cooked, stir in the cream and simmer gently for 10–15 minutes. Season with salt and pepper.

6 To serve, put the mussels into four soup plates, sprinkle with fresh thyme, then pour the hot soup over the top.

LETTUCE AND MINT SOUP

Serves 4

1 large lettuce, washed
½ tbs/15g butter
1 small onion, peeled and
    finely chopped
2 tsp chopped fresh mint
1 tbs flour
2 cups/450ml milk
⅔ cup/150 ml chicken stock (see
    page 64)
salt
freshly ground black
    pepper
5 tbs cream
mint sprigs, to garnish

1 Shred the lettuce finely.
2 Melt the butter in a large saucepan, add the lettuce, onion and chopped mint, cover and cook gently for 8–10 minutes.
3 Remove from the heat and stir in the flour. Gradually stir in the milk, stock and seasoning.
4 Return to the heat and bring to the boil, stirring continuously, then simmer very gently, half covered, for 10–15 minutes.
5 Blend or sieve the soup. Return to the rinsed saucepan, stir in the cream and heat through without boiling.
6. Serve hot or chilled, garnished with sprigs of fresh mint.

NETTLE SOUP

Nettles make a delicious soup in spring and early summer when the nettles are young and tender. Cut off the shoots from the top of the nettles, taking off about the top 2in/5cm, including the stalk and the leaves. Cut them with scissors or wear gloves to prevent the nettles from stinging you.

Serves 4–6

1 large onion, peeled and
    chopped
½ lb/225g potatoes, peeled and
    chopped
2 mint sprigs
4 cups/900 ml chicken stock (see
    page 64)
salt
freshly ground black
    pepper
juice of ½ lemon
30 nettle tops, washed

Lettuce and Mint Soup

1 Put the onion and potatoes into a large pan, along with all the remaining ingredients apart from the nettle tops.
2 Cover the pan and bring to the boil. Reduce the heat and simmer for 20 minutes.
3 Add the nettle tops to the soup and simmer gently for 1 minute.
4 Liquidize the soup, sieve it, and then return to the clean pan. Reheat and adjust the seasoning, adding a little more stock or a little milk if a thinner consistency is required. Serve hot or chilled.

ICED CUCUMBER AND MINT SOUP

Serves 4

1 large cucumber
1 small onion, peeled and
    chopped
1 small potato, peeled and
    chopped
2½ cups/625 ml chicken or vegetable
    stock (see page 64)
1 large lemon, rind and
    juice
5 mint sprigs
salt
freshly ground black
    pepper
⅔ cup/150 ml unflavoured/natural
    yogurt

1 Cut about 2in/5cm from the cucumber and reserve it for garnish. Cut the rest of the cucumber into ½in/1cm cubes, and put into a saucepan along with the chopped onion and potato.
2 Add the chicken or vegetable stock, the grated rind and juice of the lemon, one of the mint sprigs, chopped, salt and pepper.
3 Cover the pan and simmer over a low heat for 15–20 minutes, or until the cucumber and potatoes are tender.
4 Sieve or liquidize the soup, then let it cool. Stir in the yogurt and adjust the seasoning.
5 Serve the soup well chilled, garnished with thin slices of the reserved cucumber and the sprigs of mint.

CREAM OF WINTER SOUP

Serves 6

½ lb/225g potatoes, peeled and
    coarsely chopped

½ lb/225g carrots, scrubbed and
    thickly sliced
½ lb/225g parsnips (or Hamburg
    parsley roots),
    rutabagas/swedes or
    turnips, peeled and
    coarsely chopped
2 celery stalks, sliced
5 cups/1 litre chicken stock (see
    page 64)
4 sage leaves
1 bay leaf
1 parsley sprig (or top of
    Hamburg parsley)
salt
freshly ground black
    pepper

1 Put all the vegetables into a large saucepan with the stock, and add all the remaining ingredients.
2 Cover the pan and bring to the boil. Reduce the heat and simmer for 40 minutes, or until the vegetables are tender.
3 Sieve or liquidize the soup to a purée. Return it to the clean pan and reheat. Adjust the seasoning and serve hot.

POTTED HAM WITH ROSEMARY

A delicious example of the traditional English method of potting all kinds of meat, fish and game.

Serves 4

10 oz/300g cooked ham
4 tbs/50g softened butter
6 rosemary leaves, finely
    chopped
freshly ground black
    pepper
a pinch of grated nutmeg
butter or lard for sealing
1 Ogen melon, to garnish

1 Grind/mince the ham twice and put into a bowl with the softened butter.
2 Add the finely chopped rosemary leaves, and season with pepper and a little nutmeg. Blend well in a food processor.
3 Pack the seasoned meat into a dish, making sure that there are no air pockets.
4 Melt some butter or lard and gently pour over the surface to seal. As the fat begins to set you can lightly inscribe a pattern on it with the top of a knife.
5. Serve with a fan of Ogen melon slices and wholemeal bread.

SHRIMP-FILLED AVOCADOS

Serves 4

$\frac{2}{3}$ cup/150 ml unflavoured/natural yogurt
1 tsp each of fresh chopped parsley, mint, chives and lemon balm
1 small lemon
salt
freshly ground black pepper
$\frac{1}{4}$ lb/125g cooked peeled shrimp/ prawns
2 avocado pears

1 First make the filling. Put the yogurt into a mixing bowl with the herbs (if lemon balm is not available, use more parsley, chives or another lemony herb), and the juice of $\frac{1}{2}$ the lemon. Season with salt and pepper and mix well.
2 Stir in the shrimp/prawns, chopped if large, and leave to marinate for at least 30 minutes.
3 Just before serving, cut the avocado pears into halves lengthways. Remove the stones and rub the cut surfaces with the juice of the remaining $\frac{1}{2}$ lemon to prevent them turning brown.
4 Divide the filling between the avocado halves and serve.

NUT PÂTÉ

Serves 4–6

2 oz/50g bacon, chopped
$\frac{1}{2}$ lb/225g onions, peeled and chopped
1 garlic clove, peeled and crushed
1 tbs corn oil
$\frac{1}{2}$ lb/225g mixed nuts, weighed after shelling (cashews, almonds, Brazil nuts, walnuts), chopped
$\frac{1}{4}$ lb/125g fresh wholewheat bread crumbs
$1\frac{1}{2}$ tbs chopped fresh parsley
$1\frac{1}{2}$ tbs chopped fresh sage
salt
freshly ground black pepper
1 egg, beaten

1 Preheat the oven to 375°F/190°C, Gas Mark 5.
2 Fry the bacon, onions and garlic in the oil for 5 minutes, or until the onions are lightly browned.

3 Remove the pan from the heat and stir in the chopped nuts, bread crumbs, parsley, sage, salt and pepper. Stir well and then add the beaten egg. Mix together thoroughly.
4 Turn into a lightly greased 1 lb/450 g loaf pan. Alternatively, shape into a loaf on a greased baking sheet.
5 Bake for 40–45 minutes in the preheated oven, or until brown. Turn out onto a serving dish and serve immediately, or allow it to cool in the pan first and serve cold.

GAME PÂTÉ

Serves 6–8

$\frac{1}{4}$ lb/125g Canadian bacon or fat back/pork back
2 pheasants, or wild ducks, roasted
$1\frac{1}{2}$ lb/700g pork belly, ground/ minced
$\frac{1}{2}$ lb/225g pig's liver, ground/ minced
2 oz/50g fat back/pork back, diced
1 tsp grated orange rind
$1\frac{1}{2}$ tsp each of dried thyme and marjoram
1 tsp salt
1 tsp black peppercorns, coarsely crushed
$\frac{1}{4}$ cup/65 ml white wine
2 tbs brandy
clarified stock made from the cold bird carcasses (see page 64)
4 bay leaves

1 Line a 5 cup/1 litre terrine dish with the bacon or fat back.
2 Strip the meat off the game birds and chop it coarsely. Mix it with all the remaining ingredients except for the cold stock. Put the mixture into the terrine and set aside for 1 hour. Preheat the oven to 325°F/170°C, Gas Mark 3.
3 Put the terrine into a roasting pan. Half fill the pan with boiling water. Bake the pâté for $1\frac{1}{2}$–$1\frac{3}{4}$ hours, or until the top is brown and the pâté has shrunk slightly from the sides.
4 Remove the terrine from the oven and pour out any liquid. Leave to cool, then cover the top with foil and put a weight on top.
5 When the pâté is cold, pour a thin layer of the cold stock over the top, decorate with the bay leaves (and some peppercorns if you like), and refrigerate until set.

PÂTÉ WITH SPINACH AND HERBS

Serves 4–6

1 lb/450g cooked fatty pork
1 large onion, peeled
2 garlic cloves, peeled
1 lb/450g spinach, stalks removed and washed
$\frac{1}{4}$ lb/125g lamb's liver
oil or bacon drippings
$\frac{1}{4}$ lb/125g cooked pig's or lamb's tongue
1 egg, beaten
1 tbs each of dried rosemary, marjoram and tarragon
1 large bunch of parsley, chopped
$\frac{1}{2}$ tsp salt
1 tsp cayenne pepper
slices of fat back/pork back

1 Grind/mince the pork, onion and garlic together. Sweat the spinach in a saucepan until it is soft and then chop it finely.
2 Sauté the liver gently in oil or bacon drippings, then chop coarsely. Chop the tongue coarsely as well.
3 Mix all the ingredients – except for the fat back – together well.
4 Line a terrine with half the fat back slices. Stuff the pâté mixture in and cover with more fat back slices. Cover the terrine with foil, then stand it in a baking dish.
5 Pour in enough boiling water to come halfway up the sides of the terrine and bake at 375°F/190°C, Gas Mark 5 for 1 hour.
6 Let the pâté cool, then cover with a weighted plate and leave for 1 day before serving.

HERBY CHEESE DIP WITH CRUDITÉS

1½ **tbs** fresh chopped parsley
1½ **tbs** fresh chopped mint
6 oz/175g grated Cheddar cheese
3 oz/75g cottage/curd cheese
⅔ **cup/150 ml** milk
1 garlic clove, peeled and crushed
salt
freshly ground black pepper

Crudités
carrot sticks
cucumber sticks
celery chunks
scallions/spring onions
cauliflower florets
radishes
corn chips or potato chips/crisps
croûtons

1 Put the herbs and cheeses into a bowl, and beat until smooth.
2 Add the milk, garlic and seasonings, and mix again.
3 Chill well, and serve in a bowl on a plate, surrounded by a variety of crudités.

Bouillabaisse – a Mediterranean fish stew

WATER SOUCHET

Originally called sootje, *this dish was introduced from Holland at the time of William III. It is a very simple, refreshing dish and a fish dinner of Water Souchet followed by whitebait is unbeatable, particularly if it ends with a very good salad and cheese. Hot, thick, buttered toast is good with the Souchet.*

Serves 4

2	whole whiting, cleaned
1 lb/450g	whiting fillets or large fresh sardines, also filleted
½ tbs	salt
12	peppercorns
1½ cups/375 ml	white wine
¾ lb/350g	parsley, including the roots
2	lemons

1 Put the whole fish in a large saucepan with 5 cups/1 litre of water to which is added the salt and the peppercorns. Add the wine and bring to the boil. Cover the pan and simmer gently for 20 minutes.

2 Meanwhile, wash the parsley and trim the roots, keeping as much of them as possible as they add to the flavour. Chop it all finely and, reserving 1 tablespoonful for the garnish, throw the rest into the saucepan to simmer for a further 40 minutes.

3 Pour the stock through a fine strainer, reserving all the liquid. Put any nice flakes of the whole fish back into the clear green broth.

4 Put the fish fillets into a shallow pan, pour a little of the broth over them, just to cover, and poach uncovered for 5 minutes.

5 Have ready 4 heated soup bowls. Lift the fillets and lay two or more in each bowl. Pour the broth in which they cooked into the saucepan with the rest of the broth.

6 Add the juice of 1 lemon and bring to the boil. Pour through a strainer to fill up each bowl.

7 Drop a slice of the second lemon into each bowl, add a sprinkling of the reserved parsley, and serve quickly while hot.

VEGETABLE TERRINE

Any variety of green vegetables in season may be used in this recipe.

Serves 8 as a starter, 4 as a main course

4	large green cabbage leaves to line a 6in/15cm cake pan
3 cups/375g	shredded green vegetables (spinach, sorrel, Chinese cabbage, leeks, onions, scallions/spring onions)
1	egg
1	egg white
2–3 tbs	fromage blanc (or sieved cottage cheese if unavailable)
2 tbs	herbs (tarragon, chives, parsley)
	salt
	freshly ground black pepper

1 Remove the thick stalks of the whole cabbage leaves and blanch for 2–3 minutes in boiling salted water. Drain.

2 Blanch the shredded green vegetables for 2–3 minutes, then drain. (Onions and leeks may need 3–4 minutes.)

3 Line a cake pan with the cabbage leaves, the tips meeting in the centre and the base of the leaves hanging over the edge of the pan, so that they will cover the contents after the filling has been added.

4 Fill with the blanched vegetables.

5 Mix together the egg and egg white, fromage blanc, herbs and seasonings. Pour over the vegetable filling and bring up the leaves to enclose.

6 Cover with foil and bake in a *bain-marie* in a moderate oven (350°F/180°C, Gas Mark 4) for 1 hour.

7 Remove and allow to stand for 15 minutes before turning out. Slice and serve with fresh tomato sauce as a starter, or serve as an accompaniment to grilled or roast meats.

BOUILLABAISSE

MEDITERRANEAN FISH STEW

It is always difficult to know whether to classify this dish as a soup or as a stew – really it is both, as the liquid is often served as a soup, separately from the fish itself. A true bouillabaisse, they say, cannot be made away from the Mediterranean, one possible reason being that one of the most traditional ingredients – the rascasse, or scorpion fish – is not found elsewhere. For this version of bouillabaisse, use a selection of available fish – the more varied the selection, the better the dish will be.

Serves 6

4 large tomatoes, peeled and chopped
2 onions, peeled and chopped
4 garlic cloves, peeled and chopped
¾ cup/175 ml olive oil
3 parsley sprigs
2 fennel sprigs
1 bay leaf
a large pinch of saffron
salt
black pepper
5 lb/2.3 kg fish (monkfish, conger eel, red snapper, John Dory, whiting, crawfish cut into chunks; scampi and shrimps/prawns)
12 slices of French bread
1¼ cups/300 ml aïoli (see page 65)

1 Put the tomatoes, onions and garlic into a large pan with the oil. Add the herbs and the saffron and season well.
2 Put the firmer fish (monkfish and conger eel) on top and cover with boiling water. Cook over high heat for 5 minutes.
3 Now add the more tender fish (whiting, crawfish, John Dory, scampi and shrimps/prawns), and continue boiling hard for another 10 minutes.
4 Meanwhile toast the bread in a hot oven (400°F/200°C, Gas Mark 6), without letting it brown.
5 Transfer the fish to a serving dish and keep warm. Continue to boil the broth for 2 minutes longer and check the seasoning. Strain the broth.
6 Put two slices of toasted bread into each soup bowl and pour in just enough broth to moisten the bread well. Serve with the fish and the aïoli.

BUTTER BEANS HORS D'OEUVRE

Butter beans cooked with garlic and herbs make a delicious and unusual starter. You could add some chopped savory to the herb mixture.

Serves 4

½ lb/225g dried butter beans
1 large onion, peeled and chopped
1 or 2 large garlic cloves, peeled and crushed
4 tbs chopped fresh parsley
1 tbs chopped fresh thyme
1 tbs chopped fresh marjoram or oregano
1 small lemon, grated rind and juice
1 bay leaf
salt
freshly ground black pepper

1 Soak the dried beans in 2½ cups/625 ml cold water overnight – or soak in the same amount of boiling water for 2 hours.
2 Drain the beans and reserve the water. Put them into a saucepan with the onion, garlic, 3 tablespoons of parsley, the thyme and marjoram. Add the remaining ingredients and ensure they are mixed well.
3 Add enough water to bring the soaking water up to 2½ cups/625 ml, and pour it into the saucepan.
4 Cover the pan and bring to the boil. Reduce the heat and simmer for about 2 hours, or until the beans are tender, but not too soft.
5 Drain the beans, reserving the cooking liquor, and put them into a bowl. Return the cooking liquor to the pan and boil rapidly until it is reduced to about ⅔ cup/150 ml, then pour it over the beans.
6 Serve cold, sprinkled with the remaining parsley.

CHERVIL QUICHE

Serves 8 as a starter, 4 as a main course

½ **lb/225g** all-purpose/plain flour
½ **cup/125g** butter, cut into small
pieces
salt
1 egg
For the filling
1¼ **cups/300 ml** heavy/double cream or
crème fraîche
2 eggs
freshly ground black
pepper
½ **lb/225g** Emmental cheese, grated
1 large bunch of chervil,
chopped

1 Preheat the oven to 450°F/230°C, Gas Mark 8.
2 Make the pastry first. On a clean working surface, or in a bowl, mix together the flour, butter and a pinch of salt until the mixture resembles fine breadcrumbs. Break the egg over the mixture and pat together, adding a little water if necessary to obtain a supple dough.
3 Roll out the pastry and use to line a quiche pan which has been lightly greased and floured.
4 In a bowl beat the cream together with the eggs, salt and pepper. Add the cheese and chervil, and stir together thoroughly until the mixture is a consistent green colour.
5 Pour the filling into the pastry-lined quiche pan, then bake in the preheated oven for 15 minutes.
6 Lower the temperature to 350°F/180°C, Gas Mark 4 and leave to cook for a further 20 or so minutes until lightly browned.

CEVICHE

RAW FISH SALAD
Serves 6 as a starter, 4 as a main course

6 × ¼ **lb/125g** trout fillets
salt
freshly ground black
pepper
juice of 3 limes
1 small avocado pear
4 tomatoes
1 green chilli pepper
4½ **tbs** chopped fresh coriander
4 **tbs** olive oil
shredded iceberg lettuce,
to serve

1 Skin the trout fillets and cut the flesh into ½in/1cm pieces. Put into a basin and season lightly with salt and pepper. Pour over the lime juice, cover and leave to macerate in the refrigerator for at least 4 hours, or overnight.
2 Pour the lime juice into a bowl. Peel the avocado, remove the stone, and dice the flesh into ½in/1cm cubes. Add to the lime juice.
3 Peel the tomatoes, cut into quarters and remove the seeds, then chop the flesh of each into about four pieces. Halve and seed the chilli and chop the flesh very finely.
4 Add the tomatoes and chilli to the avocado, together with 3½ tablespoons of the coriander, and the olive oil.
5 Mix lightly, then add the fish and season to taste with salt and pepper. Leave in a cool place for at least 1 hour for the flavours to develop.
6 To serve, place the shredded lettuce in the base of a serving dish, spoon over the fish and vegetables, together with the liquor, and sprinkle with the reserved coriander.

Creamy Sage and Onion Flan

CREAMY SAGE AND ONION FLAN

Serves 8 as a starter, 4 as a main course

7 tbs/90g butter
2 onions, peeled and sliced
1 garlic clove, peeled and crushed
5 oz/150g whole wheat/wholemeal flour
2–3 tbs water
¼ lb/125g cottage/curd cheese, softened
⅔ cup/150 ml milk
2 eggs, beaten
1½ tbs fresh chopped sage

1 Melt 2 tablespoons of the butter and sauté the onions and garlic until soft.
2 Place the flour into a bowl, add the remaining butter in pieces, and rub into the flour until the mixture resembles fine breadcrumbs. Add the water and mix into a dough. Knead lightly and roll out on a floured work surface. Use to line a 6in/15cm quiche pan.
3 Blend the cottage/curd cheese, milk and egg, and the sage, and beat together with a fork.
4 Drain the onions and garlic, and spread over the pastry case. Pour over the cheese filling.
5 Bake in a preheated oven at 400°F/200°C, Gas Mark 6 for 40 minutes until set and golden.

TOMATO AND MINT WATER ICE

Tomato water ice, flavoured with lemon and mint, makes a refreshing and unusual start to a meal.

Serves 4

1½ lb/700g ripe tomatoes, quartered
1 small onion, peeled and chopped
½ lemon, grated rind and juice
8 large mint sprigs
2 tsp Worcestershire sauce
salt
freshly ground black pepper

1 Put the tomatoes into a saucepan with the onion and the lemon rind and juice. Add 4 sprigs of mint, the Worcestershire sauce, salt and pepper to taste.
2 Cover the pan and cook over very low heat for 10 minutes, or until the tomatoes are soft.
3 Liquidize the mixture until it is smooth, then sieve it to remove the tomato skins and seeds. Adjust the seasoning and leave to cool.
4 Pour the tomato mixture into a rigid container, cover it tightly and freeze until solid.
5 Remove the water ice from the freezer and leave it at room temperature for 15 minutes to soften slightly so that the ice can be spooned out or crushed. Pile the ice into individual bowls, garnish with the remaining sprigs of mint, and serve at once.

SORREL AND RED ONION TART

The combination of sharp, acidic sorrel and mellow cooked red onions is both colourful and unusual. This recipe can easily be adapted for small individual tarts.

½ lb/225g short/shortcrust pastry
1 egg, beaten
½ cup + 2 tbs/ 150g butter
2½ lb/1.1 kg red onions, peeled and finely sliced
½ lb/225g sorrel leaves
3 large eggs
2 cups/450 ml heavy/double cream
salt
freshly ground black pepper
a pinch of grated nutmeg

1 Line a large deep quiche pan with short/shortcrust pastry, prick the base and bake blind (with foil and beans) at 400°F/200°C, Gas Mark 6. After 20 minutes, remove and brush the base and sides of the pastry case with beaten egg. Return to the oven and bake for a further 6–7 minutes.
2 Melt ½ cup/125 g of the butter in a pan with a tight fitting lid. Add the onions and cook slowly, covered, for 30–40 minutes, stirring from time to time.
3 Remove the stalks from the sorrel leaves, wash well, and cook in a separate pan with a knob of the remaining butter, stirring constantly with a wooden spoon. Press down, but do not allow the leaves to burn. Cook until you have a thick green purée.
4 Stir the sorrel into the onions and adjust the seasoning. Spread this mixture over the base of the cooked pastry case.
5 Make a custard by beating together the eggs and cream, season with salt, pepper and nutmeg and pour over the onions.
6 Bake at 325°F/170°C, Gas Mark 3 for 45–55 minutes until the custard has set. Brush the surface with melted butter and serve with a crisp green salad which includes fresh sorrel leaves.

PAKORAS WITH MINT CHUTNEY

Pakoras are Indian fritters. They are spicy and salty and usually served with a chutney. Use any vegetable: whole spinach leaves, partially cooked cauliflower florets, thinly sliced potatoes, or onions, as here. Gram (chick-pea or lentil) flour, or besan as it is called, is available at specialist (Indian or Pakistani) food stores.

Serves 4

¼ lb/125g gram flour
1–2 tsp chilli powder
1 tsp salt
½ tsp baking powder
oil for deep-frying
4 onions, peeled
Mint chutney
1 handful of mint leaves, stalks removed
⅔ cup/150 ml unflavoured/natural yogurt
juice of 1 lemon
2 green chillies, cored and seeds removed
4 tbs desiccated coconut
1 tsp salt
½ tsp sugar

1 First make the chutney. Put all the ingredients in a liquidizer and blend until smooth. Taste and adjust the seasoning. Put in a bowl and refrigerate for 3 hours.
2 To make the fritters, sift the flour, chilli powder, salt and baking powder into a bowl. Beat in enough water to make a light batter. Heat the oil to 375°F/190°C.
3 Slice the onions and push into rings. Dip the rings into the batter individually or, alternatively, slice the onions even more thinly and mix with the batter in spoonfuls.
4 Fry the onions until brown and crisp. Drain well, and serve immediately with the chutney.

FISH AND SHELLFISH

Herbs can play a major role in fish and shellfish cookery: they can be placed in the cavity before baking; they can be burned on barbecue coals (or flamed under a fish as in the Sea Bass with Herbs Flambé); they can enliven fish stocks and court bouillons (see page 64); can complement fish when included in delicate sauces; and can be made up into cold butters (see page 65) which both garnish and flavour simultaneously.

POACHED SALMON WITH DILL SAUCE

Serves 4

4 fresh salmon steaks
1 slice of lemon or lemon rind
2–3 black peppercorns
1 bay leaf
parsley stalks
salt
freshly ground black pepper
2 tbs/25g butter
$\frac{1}{4}$ onion
6 fresh dill sprigs
$2\frac{1}{2}$ tbs heavy/double cream

1 Prepare the salmon steaks, leaving the bones in and the skin on. Keep in a damp cloth until ready to cook.

2 Make a stock using the trimmings from the fish, plus any additional bones from the fish dealer. Put bones into a large pan with the lemon slice or peel, peppercorns, bay leaf and parsley stalks. Cover with water and simmer for about 1 hour. Strain, then boil to reduce the stock by about half. Adjust the seasoning if necessary.

3 Grease a large sauté pan with a little of the butter, then add the salmon steaks. Season with salt and pepper and dot with some of the remaining butter.

4 Bring the stock to the boil and pour in enough to cover the fish. Allow the liquid to come to simmering point, by which time the fish should be just cooked. Lift out, remove the skin and bones, and keep warm.

5 Sauté the chopped onion and 2 sprigs of dill, freshly chopped, in the remaining butter.

6 Liquidize with the remaining stock and blend with the liquor in the pan. Stir in the cream and adjust the seasoning.

7 Spread a little of the sauce over each plate, lay the salmon on top, and garnish with a small sprig of dill.

Tarragon

Sea Bass with Herbs Flambé

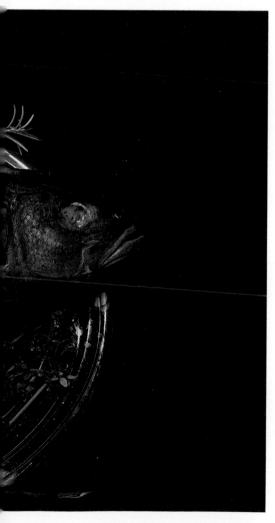

TROUT WITH LEMON TARRAGON CREAM SAUCE

Serves 2

2 fresh trout
salt
freshly ground black pepper
⅔ cup/150 ml dry white wine
1 strip of lemon rind
2 bay leaves, torn
2–3 fresh tarragon sprigs
6 black peppercorns
parsley stalks

Cream sauce
⅔ cup/150 ml heavy/double cream
1 tsp grated lemon rind
salt, pepper, sugar
½–1 tsp lemon juice
2½ tbs thick Greek yogurt
lemon slices and tarragon sprigs, to garnish

1 Clean and fillet the trout. Arrange skin side down in an ovenproof dish, season with salt and pepper, and pour the wine over.
2 Add the remaining ingredients, cover and bake in a preheated oven at 375°F/190°C, Gas Mark 5 for 15 minutes.
3 Leave to cool then strain off and retain the cooking juices. Set the fish aside.
4 For the sauce, beat the cream with the lemon rind and seasonings to taste until it is thick. Carefully whisk in as much of the cooled fish liquid as the sauce will hold without becoming thin. Add lemon juice to taste, and fold in yogurt.
5 Pour the sauce over the fish, and decorate with lemon slices and tarragon sprigs.

SEA BASS WITH HERBS FLAMBÉ

Serves 4

1 × 3 lb/1.4 kg sea bass, cleaned and gutted
2–3 tbs oil
salt
freshly ground black pepper
plenty of thyme, rosemary and fennel sprigs and stalks
3–4 tbs Pernod

1 Preheat the broiler to moderate heat.
2 Make several slits on either side of the fish. Brush it all over with the oil and season with salt and pepper.
3 Put small sprigs of the herbs into the incisions and into the gut cavity.
4 Broil the fish for about 20 minutes, turning once.
5 Place the fish on a heatproof serving dish that has been lined with sprigs and stalks of the herbs. Warm the Pernod, ignite it, and pour over the fish.

KIMBRIDGE BAKED TROUT

Serves 6–8

1 × 4 lb/1.8 kg fresh trout, cleaned with head left on
salt
freshly ground black pepper
2½ tbs lemon juice
1 oz/25g freshly grated green/root ginger
fresh parsley, chives, thyme, sage and sorrel
½ cup/125g butter

Sauce
1¼ cups/300 ml cultured sour cream
2 tbs creamed horseradish (or see page 64)
1 tbs dill seeds

1 Season the trout inside and out with salt, pepper and lemon juice. Sprinkle the fish cavity with the ginger, and stuff with available fresh herbs apart from sorrel, reserving enough for decoration.
2 Place half the butter inside the fish and lay it on a bed of sorrel leaves inside a large square of greased foil. Cover the fish with more sorrel leaves, the remaining butter in small pieces, and wrap up firmly to make a foil parcel.
3 Place on a baking sheet in a preheated oven at 375°F/190°C, Gas Mark 5 and bake for 1 hour.
4 Turn oven off and allow trout to cool in the oven for 30 minutes before removing the foil wrapping and the fish skin.
5 Serve warm, surrounded with the remaining fresh herbs, and with the sauce (simply mix all the ingredients together).

SEA BASS WITH SAFFRON, TOMATO AND PARSLEY MOUSSE

Serves 4

> 4 sea bass fillets
> 4 tomatoes
> juice of 1 lemon
> **Mousse**
> 6 oz/175g parsley
> 1 egg
> 1 egg yolk
> salt
> freshly ground black pepper
> grated nutmeg
> **Sauce**
> a pinch of saffron threads
> $\frac{2}{3}$ **cup/150 ml** white wine
> 1$\frac{1}{4}$ **cups/300 ml** fish stock (see page 64)
> $\frac{1}{2}$ Spanish onion
> $\frac{2}{3}$ **cup/150 ml** heavy/double cream
> salt
> freshly ground black pepper

1 Clean and prepare the fish. Peel, seed and dice the tomatoes.
2 Blanch the parsley leaves in boiling water, then refresh in cold water. Drain and liquidize, adding a little water if necessary, then pass through a fine sieve.
3 Blend the egg and egg yolk, and mix with the parsley purée. Season with salt, pepper and nutmeg.
4 Put the parsley mixture into four small buttered moulds and bake in a *bain-marie* in a preheated oven at 325°F/170°C, Gas Mark 3 for 30 minutes. Leave to cool, and then turn out.
5 Soak the saffron in a little hot water for 10 minutes.
6 Reduce the wine and stock with the chopped onion by about half. Add the cream, sieve, and blend in the saffron. Add a little salt and pepper to taste.
7 Put the fish fillets into a large pan, sprinkle with some salt and the lemon juice, and cover. Cook gently for 10 minutes.
8 Pour a little of the sauce onto individual serving plates, and arrange the fish on top garnished with the tomato dice, a parsley mousse, and a pastry fleuron.

Sea Bass with Parsley Mousse

MONKFISH AND SPINACH TERRINE WITH TOMATO AND BASIL SAUCE

Serves 4

> $\frac{1}{4}$ **lb/125g** spinach
> a pinch of grated nutmeg
> $\frac{1}{2}$ **lb/225g** monkfish
> 2 large egg whites
> 1 **tsp** sea salt
> $\frac{1}{2}$ **cup/125 ml** heavy/double cream
> **Sauce**
> 4 large, ripe tomatoes
> 1 garlic clove, peeled
> sea salt
> freshly ground black pepper
> 1 **tbs** olive or sunflower oil
> 4 fresh basil leaves

1 Strip the stems off the spinach, wash the leaves well and cook them gently without any added water until soft. Purée in a food processor with the nutmeg.

Salmon Mousse

2 Detach the skin, bones and any discoloured bits from the monkfish, and chop the flesh into small squares. Process with the egg whites until smooth. Add the sea salt and heavy/double cream and process again until the cream is well amalgamated. (Be careful not to overdo this stage as the mixture can curdle.)

3 Brush a small terrine or loaf pan with oil. Divide the fish mixture into three and mix one portion with the puréed spinach.

4 Spread one layer of fish over the bottom of the terrine, then the spinach layer, followed by the remaining fish.

5 Cover and place in a *bain-marie* with enough water to come half way up the sides of the terrine. Bake in a preheated oven at 300°F/160°C, Gas Mark 2 for about 15 minutes, or until set. Cool thoroughly then chill in the refrigerator before turning out.

6 To make the sauce, cut the tomatoes into six pieces each, cook quickly for 3 minutes, then sieve. Crush the garlic with a little sea salt and cook in the oil over a moderate heat for 30 seconds. Add the sieved tomato, more salt if necessary, and a little black pepper. Allow to cool, and just before serving, stir in the basil leaves torn into two or three pieces.

7 To serve, cut the terrine into thick slices and put on individual plates with a little of the sauce poured around each slice.

SALMON MOUSSE

This mousse is simplicity itself when prepared in a food processor.

Serves 6–8

1 cup/15g loosely packed fresh dill sprigs
1 cup/250ml mayonnaise (see page 65)
2 cups/500 ml unflavoured/natural yogurt
1 tbs unflavoured gelatin/gelatine powder
3 tsp lemon juice
2 slices of onion
$\frac{1}{2}$ tsp paprika
1 lb/450g canned or cooked, flaked fresh salmon
freshly ground black pepper
a dash of Tabasco sauce
1 cucumber, peeled and sliced, to garnish

1 Chop dill very finely in the processor with knife blade. Remove two-thirds of it to a small bowl and mix with half the mayonnaise and half the yogurt. Chill to serve as garnish with the cucumber slices when mousse is ready.

2 Add gelatin, lemon juice, onion, and $\frac{1}{2}$ cup/125 ml boiling water to remaining dill in the machine. Cover and process for 1 minute to dissolve the gelatin.

3 Stop machine, scrape sides with spatula, cool, then add the remaining mayonnaise and yogurt. Add remaining ingredients and process for 60 seconds.

4 Rinse a large mould in cold water but do not dry. Pour in the salmon mixture and chill overnight.

5 Serve garnished with herb mayonnaise and cucumber slices.

CRAB AND MUSHROOM MOUSSE

Serves 6 as a starter, 4 as a main course

1 × 1½ lb/700g fresh crab, cooked
6 oz/175g button mushrooms, washed, dried and chopped
1 tbs/15g butter
1 generous tbs unflavoured gelatin/gelatine powder
3 heaped tbs mayonnaise (see page 65)
4 tbs lemon juice
2 tsp English mustard
1½ tbs chopped fresh parsley
1½ tbs chopped fresh chives
1 cup/250 ml heavy/double cream
dill, parsley or watercress sprigs, to garnish

1 Remove all the meat from the crab, keeping the small claws intact. Flake the meat.

2 Turn the chopped mushrooms in the hot butter for 3 minutes, then allow to cool.

3 Measure 4 tablespoons cold water into a bowl and sprinkle the gelatin on top. Dissolve over hot water.

4 Blend the mayonnaise, lemon juice, mustard and gelatin together. Add the crab meat, mushrooms, parsley and chives and stir thoroughly, seasoning to taste with salt and pepper.

5 Whip the cream and fold it into the mixture. Turn into six small oiled moulds, or into an 8in/20cm ring mould. Chill until set.

6 Unmould the mousse and arrange on a dish, placing the claws in the centre. Garnish with sprigs of fresh dill, parsley or watercress, and serve with a crisp green salad.

Chives

FISH TERRINE WITH SMOKED EEL AND HERBS

A food processor makes light work of this complicated – but delicious – terrine.

Serves 6 as a starter, 4 as a main course

7 oz/200g halibut or monkfish fillets, skinned and boned
white wine
1 tbs chopped fresh parsley
salt
freshly ground black pepper
3 tsp unflavoured gelatin/gelatine powder

Mushroom mixture
1 tbs oil
1 garlic clove, peeled
7 oz/200g button mushrooms, quartered
1 small onion or shallot, peeled and chopped

Forcemeat
1 oz/25g each of spinach and watercress
½ oz/15g sorrel
¾ lb/350g carp or cod fillets, roughly chopped
scant ¼ lb/100g smoked eel, skinned and boned
1 egg
½ oz/15g each of fresh tarragon and chervil
1 tsp salt
⅛ tsp white pepper

1 Cut the halibut or monkfish fillets into long strips of about ¼in/6mm thick, and marinate for 1 hour in 3 tablespoons of the white wine, with the parsley, salt and pepper.

2 Heat the oil for the mushroom mixture gently in a pan with the clove of garlic. Add the mushrooms and sauté for 2 minutes. Add the onion and cook until tender. Discard garlic. Using the metal blade of the processor, blend the mushrooms and onion, and set aside.

3 For the forcemeat, blanch the spinach, watercress and sorrel together in boiling water with some salt for 1–2 minutes. Strain, refresh with cold water, and drain.

4 Still with the metal blade in the processor, place the carp fillets, eel, egg, herbs, blanched leaves, salt and pepper into the bowl, and blend to a paste.

5 Using a 1½ pint/750 ml terrine or mould, place in a layer of the carp forcemeat, ½in/1cm deep. Cover with a layer of the marinated and drained halibut or monkfish fillets, and then with a layer of the mushroom mixture. Repeat the layers until the mould is full, finishing with the carp forcemeat.

6 Cover with a sheet of oiled wax/greaseproof paper, and stand the mould in a *bain-marie*. Bake in a preheated oven at 375°F/190°C, Gas Mark 5 for 1 hour, or until the mixture is firm to the touch. Remove and cool.

7 Tilt the terrine to drain out excess liquid. Reserve, making up to 1 cup/250 ml liquid with more white wine (or water). Sprinkle on the gelatin and dissolve over gentle heat. Cool.

8 While still liquid, pour the gelatin back into the terrine to fill the sides and cover the top. Chill to set in the refrigerator.

9 To unmould, place the terrine in warm water briefly. Place a plate on top, turn terrine upside down, and shake gently onto plate. If difficult to unmould, run a knife around the inside of the terrine, keeping the blade against the sides.

10 Serve in slices with tomato and onion rings, sprinkled with a herb French dressing (see page 65), or with a fresh tomato sauce blended with fromage blanc.

HERB BAKED TROUT

Serves 2

2 fresh trout
1½ tbs each of chopped fresh parsley, tarragon, sorrel, mint, basil and coriander
2 tbs/25g butter, melted
1½ tbs chopped scallion/spring onion or shallot
juice of 1 lemon
salt
freshly ground black pepper

1 Clean and bone the trout.

2 Combine the chopped herbs with the melted butter, chopped scallion/spring onion or shallot, lemon juice and seasoning to taste.

3 Stuff each fish with the herb mixture, and place on an oiled baking sheet.

4 Cover and bake in a preheated oven at 400°F/200°C, Gas Mark 6 for 12–15 minutes. Serve immediately with the fish juices and boiled rice.

Crab and Mushroom Mousse

POULTRY AND GAME

Chicken and summer herbs are an ideal combination. Tarragon is the classic flavouring used with chicken; cold cooked chicken breasts can be coated in a creamy, herb-flecked sauce, set with reduced chicken stock and gelatin, and then decorated with whole fresh tarragon leaves. Cold cooked chicken pieces or a chicken salad welcome an accompanying herb mayonnaise or green sauce; and leftover chicken can be heated up in a cream sauce with some freshly chopped salad burnet added at the last moment. The simplest of roast chickens – or indeed a turkey – will be transformed by a herb stuffing.

Game too benefits from the fragrance of herbs – particularly if they are used in marinades.

STEAMED CHICKEN AND AVOCADO WITH TARRAGON AND VERMOUTH SAUCE

Serves 4

1 ripe avocado pear
juice of ½ lemon
4 × ½ lb/225g chicken breasts
1 tsp chopped shallot
1 tsp chopped fresh tarragon
½ cup/125g butter
1 cup/250 ml vermouth
2 cups/500 ml chicken stock
(see page 64)
1 cup/250 ml cream
salt
freshly ground black
pepper
Garnish
4 tomato roses
4 fresh marjoram sprigs

1 Quarter and peel the avocado and cut each piece lengthways into three slices. Brush with lemon juice to avoid discoloration.
2 Skin and bone the chicken breasts. Make three diagonal cuts in each one and insert the slices of avocado. Place in a steamer and cook gently for 9 minutes. Remove and keep warm.
3 Sweat the shallot and chopped tarragon in half the butter. Stir in the vermouth and reduce by two-thirds. Finally incorporate the cream and reduce until the sauce coats the back of a spoon. Blend in the remainder of the butter, a little at a time, and season to taste.
4 Coat four plates with some of the sauce, place each breast to the right of centre and garnish with a tomato and a marjoram sprig.

CHICKEN AND THYME PIE

Serves 8

1 × 2½–3 lb/
1.2–1.4 kg chicken
1 chicken liver
¾ lb/350g short/shortcrust pastry
made with whole
wheat flour
¼ lb/125g bacon
½ lemon, rind and juice
2½ tbs chopped fresh parsley
1½ tbs chopped fresh thyme
salt
freshly ground black
pepper
½ lb/225g cooked ham
1 egg
½ oz/15g unflavoured gelatin/
gelatine powder

1 Boil the chicken, reserving the chicken liver, as for chicken stock (on page 64) for about 1 hour or until tender. Allow the chicken to cool. Strain and reserve 1¼ cups/300 ml of the cooking liquid.
2 Reserve one-quarter of the pastry for the lid, and roll the rest out on a lightly floured surface. Line an 11 × 4 × 2½in/ 28 × 10 × 6cm rectangular tin. Let the excess pastry overlap the edges of the pan.
3 Cut the chicken into pieces, remove and discard the skin, and cut the meat from the bones. Coarsely chop the meat and put it into a mixing bowl.
4 Coarsely chop the bacon and the chicken liver. Add to the chicken meat with the rind and juice of the lemon, the herbs, salt and pepper. Mix well.
5 Spoon half of the chicken mixture into the pastry case. Arrange the sliced cooked ham on top then spoon in the remainder of the chicken mixture. Fold the edges of the pastry case over the filling.

6 Put the reserved pastry onto a lightly floured surface and roll it out large enough to cover the pie. Dampen the edges of the pastry case and the edges of the lid with water. Lift the lid carefully onto the pastry case. Trim the lid to fit the pie, and seal the edges well by pressing them with a fork. Cut a hole in the centre of the lid.
7 Re-roll any pastry trimmings and make leaves and a tassel for decoration. Fit the tassel into the hole in the lid and arrange the leaves at either end of the pie.
8 Brush the top of the pie with a glaze of beaten egg, and bake in a preheated oven at 400°F/200°C, Gas Mark 6, for 1 hour. If the top of the pie browns too quickly cover it with foil. Cool the pie in the tin.
9 Meanwhile, in a small saucepan, stir the gelatin into the reserved chicken stock. Heat gently until the gelatin has dissolved. When the stock is just beginning to set, remove the pastry tassel from the lid of the pie and pour in the jellied stock. Replace the tassel. Refrigerate the pie overnight.

CHICKEN LEMON SAUTÉ

Serves 4

1 × 4 lb/1.8 kg chicken, cut into pieces
salt
freshly ground black
pepper
1 tbs oil
4 tbs/50g butter
½ oz/15g flour
1 lemon, rind and juice
⅔ cup/150 ml chicken stock
(see page 64)
2 tbs dry vermouth
2 tsp chopped fresh tarragon
4 tarragon sprigs, blanched

1 Season the chicken pieces. Heat the oil and butter in a large sauté pan and sauté the chicken pieces for 8–12 minutes, until they are evenly browned. Transfer the chicken to a warmed dish and keep hot.
2 Pour off all but 1 tablespoon of the fat. Stir in the flour and cook for 2 minutes. Add the lemon juice and rind, stock, vermouth and chopped tarragon. Stir over moderate heat until the sauce has thickened.
3 Return the chicken pieces to the sauté pan. Cover the pan and simmer the chicken pieces very gently for 25–30 minutes, or until they are cooked. Test by piercing the flesh with the point of a sharp knife. If the juices run clear the chicken is cooked.
4 Transfer the chicken pieces to a warmed serving dish, strain the sauce over the chicken and garnish with the tarragon sprigs.

SAUTÉED CHICKEN WITH WINE AND MUSHROOMS

Serves 4

3 tbs/40g butter
1 tbs oil
1 × 4 lb/1.8 kg chicken, cut into serving pieces
6 oz/175g mushrooms sliced
1 shallot, chopped
$\frac{2}{3}$ cup/150 ml white wine
1$\frac{1}{4}$ cups/300 ml chicken stock (see page 64)
1 tbs tomato paste/purée
1 tbs brandy
salt
freshly ground black pepper
1 tsp finely chopped fresh tarragon
1 tsp finely chopped fresh chervil
1 tbs finely chopped fresh parsley
about 1 tbs/15g beurre manié (butter and flour mixed)

1 Heat the butter and oil in a large sauté pan and sauté the chicken pieces for 15 minutes or until they are well browned on all sides.
2 Reduce the heat and continue frying for 15 minutes. Add the mushrooms and shallot and fry, stirring, for 3–4 minutes, or until the chicken is cooked. Test by inserting the point of a sharp knife into the flesh: if the juices run clear, the chicken is cooked. Transfer the chicken

to a warmed dish and keep hot.
3 Pour the wine into the pan and bring to the boil for 1 minute. Stir in the stock, tomato paste/purée, brandy, seasoning, tarragon, chervil and 1 teaspoon of the parsley. If the sauce is too thin, stir in a little beurre manié until slightly thickened.
4 Pour the sauce over the chicken, sprinkle the remaining parsley on top, and serve.

CHICKEN KIEV

Serves 4

4 chicken breasts, skinned and boned
4 tbs/50g butter
1$\frac{1}{2}$ tbs chopped fresh parsley
2 tsp chopped fresh tarragon
2 garlic cloves, peeled and crushed
$\frac{1}{2}$ lemon, rind and juice
salt
freshly ground black pepper
seasoned flour
1 egg, beaten
$\frac{1}{4}$ lb/125g dry bread crumbs
oil for deep-frying
Garnish
1 lemon, quartered
1 bunch of watercress, washed

1 Place the chicken breasts between two pieces of cellophane, and flatten with a mallet or rolling pin.
2 Cream the butter in a mixing bowl. Beat in the herbs, garlic, grated lemon rind and seasoning and moisten with a teaspoon of the lemon juice. Shape the butter into a rectangle and chill in the refrigerator until firm.
3 Cut the chilled butter in four equal pieces and put one piece in the centre of each flattened chicken breast. Roll up tightly, folding in the edges so that the butter is completely encased, and secure each roll with a cocktail stick.
4 Coat the chicken rolls first with flour, then with egg, and lastly with the bread crumbs. Put on a plate and chill in the refrigerator for at least 1 hour.
5 Heat the oil to 375°F/190°C. Fry the chicken rolls for about 7 minutes or until they are golden. Drain well.
6 Transfer to a warmed platter, garnish with the lemon wedges and watercress, and serve.

Sage

LEMON AND HERB BAKED CHICKEN

Serves 4

4 chicken breasts
2 medium onions, peeled and finely chopped
1 large lemon, rind and juice
4$\frac{1}{2}$ tbs chopped fresh parsley
1$\frac{1}{2}$ tbs chopped fresh thyme
1$\frac{1}{2}$ tbs chopped fresh sage
1$\frac{1}{2}$ tbs chopped fresh mint
salt
freshly ground black pepper
$\frac{2}{3}$ cup/150 ml chicken stock (see page 64)

1 Preheat the oven to 350°F/180°C, Gas Mark 4.
2 Put the chicken breasts into an ovenproof dish or a small roasting pan and bake, uncovered, for 30 minutes.
3 Meanwhile, mix the finely chopped onion with the grated lemon rind and juice and the herbs. Season with salt and pepper.
4 Remove the chicken from the oven and pour off any fat that is in the pan. Pour the well seasoned stock over the chicken, and press the herb mixture on top of the chicken breasts.
5 Return the chicken to the oven and bake for 15–20 minutes, or until the herb topping is crisp and lightly browned. Serve hot or cold.

Marjoram

ROAST CHICKEN

A plainly roasted chicken is traditionally accompanied by bacon rolls and tiny sausages, but it can also have a variety of stuffings to ring the changes. Try mixing together 4 tbs/50 g butter, a crushed garlic clove, some lemon juice, salt and pepper, and 2 tbs of a chopped herb – tarragon, watercress, sage, chervil, fennel, or a combination of celery leaves and lemon thyme. Place inside the cavity and baste the chicken with the fragrant juices as they run out. The stuffing could be more substantial, using about $\frac{1}{2}$ lb/ 225 g sausage meat, 2 oz/50 g fresh bread crumbs, a finely chopped onion, some herbs of choice and seasoning. Calculate the cooking time on the weight of the chicken plus the stuffing (20 minutes per lb/450 g, and up to 20 minutes over).

Roast Chicken and Raised Game Pie

Serves 4

1 × 4 lb/1.8 kg chicken, giblets reserved
2 tbs/25g dripping or bacon fat
salt
freshly ground black
 pepper
6 slices bacon
1 onion, peeled and sliced
1 carrot, scrubbed and
 sliced
thyme and marjoram

1 Preheat the oven to 375°F/190°C, Gas Mark 5 and melt the dripping in a roasting pan. Season the chicken with salt and pepper and cover the breast with the bacon slices. Place in the pan, baste well and put in the oven.

2 Roast for the required time – a good hour approximately – removing the bacon for the last 30 minutes so that the breast will brown. Meanwhile, make a giblet stock with the giblets, onion, carrot, herbs and 2 cups/500 ml water.

3 Test to see whether the chicken is cooked. Pierce with the point of a sharp knife; if the juices run clear, the chicken is ready. Transfer it to a warmed dish and keep hot.

4 Pour off most of the fat from the roasting pan, and strain in the giblet stock. Place over heat and boil, stirring in all the sediment, until the gravy is reduced and well flavoured. If you prefer the gravy thicker, stir in 1 teaspoon flour mixed with a little water, and cook until the gravy has thickened. Pour into a gravy boat.

RAISED GAME PIE

Serves 8

2 lb/900g mixed game
¾ lb/350g hot-water crust pastry
¼ lb/125g bacon
1 lb/450g sausage meat
¼ lb/125g mushrooms, sliced
salt
freshly ground black
 pepper
2½ tbs chopped fresh thyme,
 sage and marjoram
1 egg, beaten
⅔ cup/150 ml well-flavoured aspic

1 Preheat the oven to 400°F/200°C, Gas Mark 6. Remove the flesh from the game and cut into strips.

2 Line a greased pie mould with the hot-water crust pastry dough, saving a third of the dough for the lid.

3 Put the bacon in a layer at the bottom of the pie case. Cover with a layer of sausage meat then layer the game, the rest of the sausage meat and the mushrooms. Season well between each layer and sprinkle with the herbs.

4 Roll out the remaining dough to make the lid. Dampen the edges of the dough and cover the pie. Press to seal, trim and decorate, and brush with the beaten egg. Make a hole in the centre of the lid.

5 Bake for 30 minutes in the preheated oven, then reduce the temperature to 300°F/150°C, Gas Mark 2 and bake for another 1½ hours. Remove the pie from the oven and allow to cool.

6 Heat the aspic just enough to melt it and pour it into the pie through a funnel placed in the steam vent. Chill the pie for at least 6 hours before serving.

GUINEA FOWL WITH SCALLIONS AND SWEET HERBS

Serves 4

2 guinea fowl
salt
freshly ground black
 pepper
a large bunch of "sweet"
 herbs (thyme,
 marjoram, parsley,
 chervil etc)
1 large onion, peeled and
 chopped
8 scallions/spring onions
1 tbs/15g butter
juice of ½ lemon

1 First divide up the guinea fowl. Fillet the breasts from the birds, cut off the wings and remove the legs and thighs, which can be divided at the joint. Use the carcass to make stock (see page 64).

2 Cut a slit in the inside of the legs, rub with salt and pepper, and insert some chopped herbs. Put the legs, thighs and wings into a well buttered ovenproof dish and cook in a preheated oven at 400°F/200°C, Gas Mark 6 for about 25 minutes.

3 Line a separate dish with chopped onion and some more chopped herbs, and lay the breasts on top. Season and cook in a cooler part of the oven (towards the foot), for 10–15 minutes, basting the skin several times.

4 To make the sauce, reduce the stock in a pan and add some of the juices from the meat. Adjust the seasoning and cook until the sauce is smooth and syrupy.

5 Put a little of the sauce on each plate and arrange the wing and leg pieces of the guinea fowl on it. Cut the scallions/spring onions diagonally and toss lightly in butter with some more chopped herbs and lemon juice.

6 Spread some of this mixture on each plate and top with strips of breast meat sliced lengthways. Decorate with a few sprigs of fresh herbs.

MEAT

Different herbs have different affinities with different meats, and there is no meat that would not be complemented by a herb used in the cooking or in an accompanying sauce. Even a herb butter sauce or a pat of a herb butter can transform a simple fried or broiled piece of meat.

Hot roast beef, for instance, is traditionally associated with the hot pungency of horseradish, but cold roast or boiled beef or beef salads can be spiked with the flavours of dill or a mixture of herbs in a mayonnaise or French dressing.

Veal, a blander meat, needs more flavour: sage and thyme are good, but a sorrel sauce can lift the plainest piece of veal.

Roast lamb is served in the UK with a mint sauce – a usage the French cannot sanction – but a mint crust (mint mixed with butter and bread crumbs and pressed onto the joint) is another way of adding that complementary flavour. Rosemary and garlic are good with lamb too; place slivers of garlic or sprigs of rosemary in small slits in the skin, or roast the lamb on top of rosemary sprigs.

Pork, a rich meat, goes well with sage, dill, savory and hyssop, all herbs which can help to counteract the fattiness. Its traditional accompaniment, a tart apple sauce, fulfils the same function. And gammon, ham or bacon are ideally partnered by parsley – in a simple white sauce or, cold, set in a green parsley jelly.

Made-up meat dishes can all benefit from the use of herbs. The meat for stews or casseroles can be vastly improved if marinated first in a herb marinade; so too, can meats for broiling (chops, steaks and kebabs). Meatballs and meat loaves are all made tastier by the addition of herbs – try mint in the former, thyme, marjoram or lovage in the latter.

LEMON AND HERB FILLET STEAKS

Serves 4

4 × ½ lb/225g beef fillet steaks
salt
1 tbs black peppercorns, crushed
grated rind of ½ lemon
2½ tbs chopped fresh herbs (basil, parsley, chives etc)
4 tbs/50g butter

1 Lightly season the steaks with salt.
2 Mix together the peppercorns, lemon rind and herbs, and spread the mixture evenly over both sides of each steak. Leave to stand for 30–60 minutes.
3 Fry the steaks in the butter to taste, and serve with the cooking juices poured over the top.

Gammon with Parsley Sauce

MEAT LOAF

Serves 6

1½ lb/700g lean beef, ground/minced
1 large onion, peeled and
finely chopped
3 garlic cloves, peeled and
finely chopped
1½ tbs olive oil
2½ tbs chopped fresh lovage
salt
freshly ground black
pepper
2 slices of brown bread,
crusts removed

1 Put the ground beef into a bowl, and add the onion, garlic, oil, lovage, salt and pepper to taste.
2 Soak the bread in water for 5–10 minutes (or milk if preferred), then squeeze as dry as possible. Add to the beef mixture.
3 Mix all the ingredients together very thoroughly with the hands.
4 Put the mixture into a greased 2 lb/900 g loaf pan, cover with foil, and bake in a preheated oven at 350°F/180°C, Gas Mark 4 for 1½ hours.
5 Turn out onto a serving dish. Serve hot or cold in slices.

GAMMON WITH PARSLEY AND MUSHROOM SAUCE

Serves 4

4 gammon steaks
2 tomatoes, halved
decoratively
1 oz/25g flour
2 tbs/25g butter
2½ cups/600 ml milk
2½ tbs chopped fresh parsley
freshly ground black
pepper
6 oz/175g button mushrooms,
sliced

1 Snip the gammon rind edges at 1in/2.5cm intervals. Broil with the tomatoes, turning once.
2 Place the flour, butter and milk in a pan, and heat, stirring continuously, until the sauce thickens and is smooth.
3 Add the remaining ingredients and simmer gently for 5 minutes.
4 Arrange the gammon steaks on a serving plate. Cover with a little sauce and garnish with tomatoes. Serve remaining sauce separately.

Pork Fillet Wellington

PORK FILLET WELLINGTON

Serves 4–6

2 tbs/25g butter
2 pork fillets
1 small onion, peeled and
chopped
3 slices bacon, chopped
½ lb/225g mushrooms, chopped
1½ tbs mixed fresh herbs
(or 1½ tsp dried)
freshly ground black
pepper
1½ tbs chopped fresh parsley
12 oz/350g puff pastry
1 egg, beaten

1 Heat the butter in a large frying pan and brown the pork fillets on all sides. Set aside to cool.
2 Add the onion, bacon and mushrooms to the fat remaining in the pan, season with herbs and black pepper, and cook for 3 minutes. Stir in the parsley, then leave to cool.
3 Roll out the pastry so that it is large enough to encase both fillets of pork. Place them in the centre of the pastry, top them with the mushroom mixture, then cover with the pastry. Press to seal, using the beaten egg to seal and glaze the pastry. Decorate with pastry leaves if you like.
4 Place on a baking sheet and bake in a preheated oven at 450°F/230°C, Gas Mark 8 for 10 minutes. Reduce the heat to 400°F/200°C, Gas Mark 6 and continue baking for about 30 minutes. Serve in slices.

SALTIMBOCCA

Serves 4

8 thin, veal scallops/
escalopes, about
3in/7.5cm across
salt
freshly ground
black pepper
8 sage leaves
8 slices Parma ham, the
same size as the veal
4 tbs/50g butter
4 tbs white wine

1 Flatten the veal well. Season lightly with salt and pepper.
2 Put a sage leaf and then a slice of ham on top of each piece of veal. Roll and secure with a cocktail stick.
3 Heat the butter in a large frying pan. When foaming, add the rolls and fry briskly on all sides for 6–8 minutes, or until they are cooked through.
4 Transfer the scallops/escalopes to a warmed dish and keep hot.
5 Stir the wine into the juices in the pan and bring to the boil, scraping and stirring. Pour over the escalopes.

GREEN PORK AND GREEN DUMPLINGS

Serves 6–8

4–5 lb/2–2.5 kg top leg of pork, scored
for crackling
1 tbs seasoned flour
¾ cup/175g butter (or ¾ cup dripping)
potatoes for roasting
Forcemeat
2 cups/ 250g fine white fresh
bread crumbs
1 cup/125g shredded suet
1 tbs finely chopped fresh sage
1 tsp dried oregano
4 tbs finely chopped fresh
parsley
salt
freshly ground black
pepper
1 egg
a little milk, if required
Green dumplings
¾ cup/90g shredded suet
1 cup/125g flour
2 tbs very finely chopped fresh
parsley
1 tbs finely chopped fresh
thyme, sage,
marjoram, chives and
tarragon (not mint)
½ tsp salt
¼ tsp freshly ground black
pepper
¼ lb/125g cooked spinach (or
thawed frozen spinach)

1 Slash the pork in four of the scores
which the butcher has made for
crackling, to a depth of 2–3in/5–7.5cm.
Additionally, cut just beneath the skin
through the thin layer of fat on top of
the meat to lift a flap about 3in/7.5cm
long on top of the joint.
2 Make the forcemeat by mixing the
bread crumbs, suet, sage, oregano, half
the parsley, half teaspoon of salt and a
good pinch of black pepper. Break the
egg into the mixture and stir and beat
well. If the mixture is too dry to
amalgamate, add a little milk.
3 Pull the cuts in the meat well open and
stuff as much forcemeat as possible
inside. Spread all the remaining
forcemeat in the opening and between
meat and skin.
4 Rub the whole joint with the seasoned
flour. Put the meat in a baking pan with
the butter and plenty of potatoes. Put the
baking pan in a preheated hot oven (at
400°F/200°C, Gas Mark 6).
5 After an hour baste the meat and
potatoes. If the crackling is becoming

dark, reduce the heat to 350°F/180°C,
Gas Mark 4. Bake for 1 more hour.
6 Meanwhile, prepare the dumplings.
Stir the suet into the flour with the herbs,
salt and pepper. Press about 6
tablespoons of juice from the cooked
spinach (or pour off the water from
frozen spinach and then press it well).
Stir the green liquid into the flour
mixture to make a stiff dough and knead
it a little. Divide the dough to make
walnut-sized balls (about twelve). Set
aside in a cool place.
7 About 10 minutes before the
dumplings are to be eaten, have about 5
cups/1 litre of salted water boiling in a
large saucepan. Drop the dumplings in
and boil briskly (but not so hard that
they will break up). Do not let the water
go off the boil. Lift the little green balls
out with a perforated spoon.
8 Remove the joint to a large dish and
surround with the dumplings. Put the
roast potatoes in a separate dish and
sprinkle thickly with the remaining
parsley.
9 Serve with some cooked peas, cabbage
or spinach, accompanied by a good
gravy, and some gooseberry or apple
sauce.

Right: Marinated Pork Chops
Below: Lamb Medallions with Tarragon

MARINATED PORK CHOPS

Serves 4

6 pork loin chops
Marinade
5 tbs olive oil
1 lemon, rind and juice
1½ tbs chopped fresh parsley
1 tsp each of chopped fresh
thyme, sage and
oregano
salt
freshly ground black
pepper
4 bay leaves
1 garlic clove, peeled and
crushed

1 Trim the outer fat from the chops and
remove the bones.
2 Mix together all the marinade
ingredients and pour into a shallow dish.
Marinate the chops for about 4–5 hours.
3 Thread the chops onto long skewers,
or place on the rack of the broiler.
4 Place under a preheated broiler and
cook for about 10 minutes on each side.
The chops can also be cooked on a
barbecue, or in the oven on a bed of
vegetables (at 400°F/200°C, Gas Mark 6)
for 45 minutes.

LAMB MEDALLIONS WITH TARRAGON

Serves 4

8 medallions of lamb,
about 1½in/3cm thick
salt
freshly ground black
pepper
3 tbs oil
4 tbs/50g butter
6 tbs Madeira wine
2 tbs finely chopped fresh
tarragon
4 tbs heavy/double cream

1 Trim the medallions and season.
2 Heat the oil with half the butter in a
large sauté pan and brown the meat for
5–10 minutes on each side – or to taste.
Arrange the meat on a warmed serving
dish.
3 Add the remaining butter to the pan,
along with the Madeira, tarragon and
cream, and heat until just below boiling
point. Pour over the lamb.

BEEF FILLET IN PUFF PASTRY WITH MUSTARD AND CHERVIL SAUCE

It is important to use the best fillet of beef – either from the head or tail end – for this recipe, because of its tenderness.

Serves 4

> 1½ lb/700g beef fillet
> 1 lb/450g puff pastry
> 1 egg, beaten with a little water
> salt
> freshly ground black pepper
> 2 tbs/25g butter
>
> **Sauce**
> ½ Spanish onion, peeled and finely chopped
> chervil stalks
> ½ cup/125 ml dry white wine
> 1¼ cups/300 ml strong beef, chicken or veal stock (see pages 63 and 64)
> 2 good tbs Dijon mustard
> ⅔ cup/150 ml heavy/double cream
> 1 bunch of chervil, finely chopped

1 Trim the meat and cut into cubes. Put to one side.

2 Roll out the puff pastry thinly and cut into eight equal squares. Cut the centre out of four of these pieces.

3 Place the "frames" over the four intact squares, moisten the rims with water and press together. Glaze the tops with the egg and water mixture. Lightly score a criss-cross pattern on the cut-out centres of the frames (these form the lids).

4 Bake the pastry in a preheated hot oven at 425°F/220°C, Gas Mark 7 for 10–15 minutes, allowing slightly less time for the lids.

5 To make the sauce, boil together the onion, chervil stalks, wine and stock until reduced by three-quarters. Salt lightly to test the strength of the flavour and reduce further if necessary. Add the mustard and cream and adjust the seasoning. Pass through a sieve and add the finely chopped chervil leaves.

6 Season the beef fillet with salt and pepper, and sauté very quickly in hot butter, shaking the pan and turning the meat. After about 1 minute remove and use to fill the four pastry cases. Finally pour around the sauce and serve.

ROAST BELLY OF PORK WITH ROSEMARY POTATOES

Serves 6

> 2–2½ lb/ 1–1.25 kg lean end belly of pork
> salt
> freshly ground black pepper
> 8 fresh rosemary sprigs (or lots of dried rosemary pieces)
> 2½ lb/1.25 kg potatoes, scrubbed and sliced thickly
> 2 onions, peeled and sliced
> oil

1 Remove the rind from the pork, set aside, and season the top of the meat well.

2 Lay two sprigs of rosemary in the bottom of the roasting pan, place the pork on them and place two more sprigs on top. Cook in a preheated oven at 325°F/160°C, Gas Mark 3 for 1¼ hours.

3 Remove the pork, place in another roasting pan, and keep warm. Turn the oven temperature up to 400°F/200°C, Gas Mark 6.

Roast Belly of Pork

4 Mix the potatoes and onion in the pork roasting pan. Cover with the remaining sprigs of rosemary. Place the pork and the potatoes in the oven, the potatoes at the top, and cook for a further hour, turning the potatoes over occasionally.

5 Brush the pork rind with oil and salt and cook in the oven on the top shelf for the last 15 minutes.

6 Serve the potatoes and onion separately, to accompany the sliced pork, with pieces of the crackling as a garnish.

STEAMED BEST END OF LAMB WITH ROSEMARY

Serves 4

1 pair	best ends of lamb
½	garlic clove, peeled and crushed
1	thyme sprig
1	rosemary sprig
½	onion, peeled and chopped
1	carrot, scrubbed and sliced

1 Remove the meat from the bone and trim off all the sinew and fat. Then pare off the fat and chop it into small pieces.

2 Place the bones and fat and all the other ingredients (crushed garlic, herbs, chopped onion and sliced carrot) into a large pan. Cover with cold water, bring to the boil, and simmer for about 45 minutes. Remove any foam.

3 Strain off the stock, leave to cool, and skim off all the fat as it rises to the surface. Bring to the boil and reduce until there is about 2½ cups/600 ml of liquid left. This is the liquid used for steaming the lamb.

4 Put the meat on a steaming rack over the reduced stock, and steam for about 10 minutes.

5 Serve sliced on a bed of root vegetables and pour over the juices and liquor used for the steaming. Rosemary jelly (see page 109) complements this dish well.

LAMB KORMA

Serves 4

2 tbs/25g	butter
1	onion, peeled and chopped
2	garlic cloves, peeled and crushed
2in/5cm	piece of fresh green/root ginger, grated
2 tsp	ground coriander
2 tsp	ground cumin
1 tsp	ground turmeric
½ **tsp**	ground cinnamon
1 lb/450g	lamb (leg or shoulder), cubed
2 oz/50g	cashew nuts
1¼ cups/300 ml	unflavoured/natural yogurt
2½ tbs	chopped fresh coriander mint leaves, to garnish

1 Melt the butter in a large saucepan, and sauté the onion and garlic until soft.

2 Add the ginger and spices, and continue frying gently for a few minutes longer.

3 Add the cubes of lamb, the nuts, yogurt and chopped coriander. Cook on a low heat, covered, for 30 minutes.

4 Serve garnished with mint leaves, and accompanied by Basmati rice, a cucumber and mint *raita* (see page 95) and poppadums.

Lamb Korma

EGGS AND PASTA

Eggs are ideal partners for herbs, as their blandness – both in their taste and the way they look – is offset by the freshness, flavour and colour of herbs. Buttered or scrambled eggs gain onion flavour by a sprinkling of chives (try some slivers of smoked salmon as well for a more luxurious dish); and omelettes with herbs are tasty. Poached eggs can be served on a herb or vegetable purée – try sorrel, nettle or potato flecked with plenty of fresh herbs; and baked eggs can be flavoured with herbs, particularly tarragon. In fact eggs for poaching or boiling can be flavoured *before* cooking: wrap fresh raw eggs in fresh tarragon leaves and then foil or film; leave in a cool place for 24 hours and then cook in the normal way, when the egg will have absorbed the flavour of the herb. Hard-boiled eggs can be served in a creamy herb sauce or mayonnaise, and can be stuffed with a herb filling.

The Italians use herbs in much of their cooking, and their pasta dishes are no exception. Oregano is perhaps the herb most associated with pizza toppings, and the basil *pesto* sauce served with spaghetti or noodles is justly world famous. Try pasta too with a tomato and basil sauce or tossed in a simple herb butter sauce. (A chopped herb could perhaps be discreetly mixed into the basic pasta dough.) Ravioli with a ricotta filling could be flavoured with a number of herbs, as could a meat filling – and gnocchi, made from potato, cheese or polenta, could be coloured green by the addition of chopped herbs such as sorrel, watercress, parsley, chervil, tarragon or dill.

PIZZA NAPOLETANA

Makes 2 pizzas

½ oz/15g fresh yeast
¼ tsp sugar
½ cup/125 ml lukewarm water
½ lb/225g all-purpose/plain white flour
½ tsp salt
2 tbs olive oil

Topping
8 medium tomatoes, blanched, skinned and chopped
salt
freshly ground black pepper
8 thin slices mozzarella cheese
8 anchovy fillets
6 black olives, halved and pitted
1 tsp chopped fresh oregano
1 tsp chopped fresh basil
2 tsp olive oil

1 Put the yeast, sugar and 2 tablespoons of the water into a small bowl and mash the mixture with a fork to make a smooth paste. Set the bowl aside in a warm draught-free place for about 15 minutes or until the mixture is puffed up and frothy.
2 Sift the flour and salt into a bowl and make a well in the centre. Pour in the yeast mixture, the remaining water and about two-thirds of the oil. Mix the liquids together, gradually incorporating the flour. Mix the dough with your hands until it begins to leave the sides of the bowl.
3 Turn the dough out onto a lightly floured surface and knead it for about 10 minutes, or until it is smooth and elastic.
4 Rinse, dry and lightly grease the mixing bowl. Shape the dough into a ball and place it in the bowl. Cover with a damp cloth and set aside in a warm, draught-free place for about 1 hour, or until the dough has doubled in bulk.
5 Turn the dough out onto the work surface again and knead it for 3 minutes. Divide the dough in half and shape each half into a ball. Flatten each ball by pressing down with the heel of your hand until it forms a circle about ¼in/6mm thick. Brush the top of the dough with the remaining oil.
6 Heat the oven to 450°F/230°C, Gas Mark 8, and lightly grease a large baking sheet. Place the two dough circles on the sheet.
7 Put half the tomatoes on each pizza and sprinkle with a little salt and lots of black pepper. Put four slices of cheese on each pizza and garnish with the anchovies and olives. Sprinkle over the herbs and moisten with the olive oil.
8 Bake the pizzas for about 20 minutes, or until the cheese has melted and is bubbling. Serve hot or cold.

BUTTERED EGGS WITH HERBS

Serves 2

4 eggs
salt
freshly ground black pepper
3 tbs/40g butter
2 slices of hot buttered toast
3 tbs chopped chives

RAVIOLI WITH RICOTTA

Freshly made, these delicate little "cushions" of pasta are superb. Cottage/curd cheese may be substituted for the Ricotta, and fresh dill could be used instead of the marjoram.

Serves 4

> ½ lb/225g flour
> ½ tsp salt
> 2 eggs
> **Filling**
> ½ lb/225g ricotta cheese
> 2 oz/50g grated Parmesan cheese
> ½ tsp dried marjoram
> ¼ tsp ground nutmeg
> 1 egg
> freshly ground black pepper

1 Mix the flour with the salt on a large board or working surface, and make a well in the centre.
2 Beat the eggs with 2 tablespoons of water in a bowl, then pour into the well in the flour. Using your hands, gradually draw the flour into the egg mixture until a stiff dough is obtained, adding up to 2 tablespoons more of water if necessary.
3 Knead the dough for about 10 minutes, or until it is smooth and elastic.
4 Place on a lightly floured surface and divide in two. Roll each half out very thinly to form a rectangle about 14 × 12in/35 × 30cm. Leave the dough to rest for 15 minutes.
5 Meanwhile, mix the ricotta cheese thoroughly with half the Parmesan, the marjoram, nutmeg, egg, and salt and pepper to taste.
6 Brush one-half of the pasta with water. At 2in/5cm intervals, put 1 teaspoon of the ricotta mixture. Cover with the other half of the pasta and seal by pressing along the edges and between the mounds of ricotta filling. Using a 2in/5cm fluted pastry cutter, cut round each mound or cut into squares (about 28). Leave the ravioli to dry for 10 minutes before cooking it.
7 Add the ravioli to a large pan of boiling salted water and cook for 5 minutes, or until it is just tender. Drain and put into a hot serving dish.
8 Sprinkle with the remaining Parmesan cheese (and with some finely chopped parsley too, if you like), and serve immediately.

1 Break the eggs into a bowl and season well. Using a fork, lightly beat the eggs until the whites and yolks are blended.
2 Melt half the butter over low heat and pour in the eggs. Using a wooden spoon, and keeping the heat low, stir the eggs, pulling the large curds from the base of the pan. At the same time add the remaining butter, a little at a time.
3 When almost all the egg has formed moist curds, remove the pan from the heat, and stir until cooked and creamy, Place on top of the toast and sprinkle with the chives. Serve immediately, by itself, or accompanied by a green salad for a light lunch.

Spaghetti with Pesto and Ravioli with Ricotta

OMELETTE AUX FINES HERBES

Fines herbes – a mixture of finely chopped chervil, chives, parsley and, occasionally, tarragon – are a classic flavouring for an omelette, but herbs on their own can be used as well: try puréed sorrel, for instance.

Serves 2

> 5 eggs
> sea salt
> freshly ground black pepper
> 2 tbs/25g butter
> 2 tbs finely chopped fresh herbs (as above, or to taste)

1 Break the eggs into a bowl and season well. Using a fork, lightly beat the eggs until the whites and yolks are well blended.
2 Melt the butter in a hot omelette pan, swirling it around the base and sides. When it foams, pour in the eggs and shake the pan gently backwards and forwards.
3 After a moment's cooking, sprinkle on most of the herbs.
4 Draw the cooked edges of the omelette up with a spatula, allowing the uncooked eggs to run underneath.
5 When set but still soft on the top, tilt the pan and slide the omelette out onto a hot dish. Divide in two and sprinkle the top with the remaining herbs.

SPAGHETTI WITH PESTO

Serves 4

> 1 handful of fresh basil, washed and chopped
> 2 oz/50g pine nuts/kernels
> 2 garlic cloves, peeled
> 2 oz/50g grated Parmesan cheese
> ⅔ cup/150 ml olive oil
> 1 lb/450g spaghetti
> 4 tbs/50g butter

1 Blend the basil, nuts/kernels and garlic in a liquidizer to form a smooth paste (or use a pestle and mortar).
2 Add the cheese and then, with the liquidizer at low speed, drip the oil in very slowly, making sure that it is binding with the paste before adding more.
3 Cook the spaghetti, drain it and transfer it to a hot serving dish.
4 Toss the spaghetti with the butter and the pesto sauce and serve immediately.

VEGETABLES AND SALADS

Fresh herbs transform vegetables and salads, and many indeed have a traditional association – mint with fresh young vegetables, basil with tomatoes, dill with potatoes, savory with beans, sage with onions. A chosen herb can be cooked with a vegetable, added to a simple butter sauce – and can even make a sauce in itself as in the case of sorrel or nettles. A purée of a root vegetable can be transformed both visually and taste wise by a sprinkling of a herb (try some lovage); baked tomatoes by a pat of herb butter; your favourite ratatouille recipe by a last-minute tucking in of some basil leaves. Vegetables can be stuffed with a herb mixture: try the pepper and cucumber recipes on the following pages, as well as tomatoes stuffed with cream cheese and some chopped salad burnet.

Rice, too, whether as a hot accompaniment or as a salad, benefits from the addition of herbs, as will other grains such as millet and buckwheat – the famous Middle Eastern *tabbouli*, for instance. Salads in general will all appreciate herbs, many herbs indeed forming a major ingredient – salad burnet, rocket and sorrel, for example. Try tomato salads with basil and mozzarella cheese, with scallions/spring onions and chopped rocket.

Dress all salads with a herb dressing, or with a herb mayonnaise (see page 65). Use garlic in dressings: actually crushed into the dressing for a strong flavour; merely rubbed round the salad bowl for a lighter flavour. Another way to flavour a salad with garlic is to make a *chapon*. Rub a slice of stale French bread all over with a bruised garlic clove. Drop it in among the salad greens shortly before tossing them. Soaked with dressing, a *chapon* is a delicacy in its own right.

POTATO SALAD

You can mix in about ⅔ cup/150 ml mayonnaise (see page 65) and about 1 tbs creamed horseradish after adding the potato to the French dressing.

Serves 4

1½ lb/700g potatoes, peeled
⅔ cup/150 ml herb French dressing (see page 65), made with chives
1 bunch of scallions/spring onions, chopped
1 tbs chopped fresh parsley

1 Boil the potatoes until just tender, then peel them while still hot.
2 Place the French dressing into a serving bowl, and cut the potatoes up into the bowl. Turn while they cool.
3 Add the scallions/spring onions, leave until cold and serve chilled, scattered with the parsley.

ENGLISH POTATO AND PARSLEY PATTIES

Serves 4

1 lb/450g potatoes, scrubbed
1 tbs bacon fat
1 large handful of parsley, finely chopped
salt
freshly ground black pepper
flour
oil

1 Boil the potatoes until tender, and then peel them. Mash them with the dripping and the parsley, and salt and pepper to taste. The parsley should turn the whole mass bright green.
2 Form the mixture into small spheres, flatten into patties, and dip into flour.
3 Fry in minimum oil until browned and crisp on the outside.

MILLET CROQUETTES

Makes 6 croquettes

¼ lb/125g millet
1 onion, peeled and finely chopped
oil
1½ tbs chopped fresh mixed herbs
salt

1 Boil the millet in 1½ cups/375 ml water until all the water is absorbed and the grains form a solid mass.
2 Fry the onion in a very little oil until it is soft. Toss in the herbs and stir-fry for 30 seconds.
3 Mix the millet with the onion, herbs and a pinch of salt, and form into six balls. Flatten them into cakes about ¾in/2cm thick.
4 Brown on both sides on a lightly oiled griddle.

POTATO STICKS

½ lb/225g potatoes, peeled
salt
4 tbs/150g butter
2 egg yolks
¼ lb/125g self-rising/self-raising
flour
freshly ground black
pepper
1½ tbs chopped fresh chives
1 egg, beaten
sesame seeds

1 Cook the potatoes in boiling salted water until tender. Drain and mash with the butter and egg yolks until creamy.
2 Beat in the flour, more salt, pepper and chives to form a dough. Chill in the refrigerator for at least 30 minutes.
3 Roll out into a rectangle of about ½in/ 1cm thick. Cut into sticks ½in/1cm wide and 2¼in/6cm long. Twist and brush lightly with beaten egg.
4 Place on a greased baking sheet, sprinkle with sesame seeds, and bake in a preheated oven at 400°F/200°C, Gas Mark 6 for 10 minutes, or until golden brown and crisp. Leave on the sheet until cool.

STUFFED CUCUMBER

Serves 4–6

1 large cucumber, peeled
and cut crossways into
pieces
¼ lb/125g canned tuna fish
1 tbs/15g butter
1 oz/25g cream cheese
1½ tbs chopped fresh parsley
1 tsp each of chopped fresh
thyme, oregano,
tarragon and chives
½ tsp lemon juice
salt
freshly ground black
pepper

1 Using a sharp knife or a teaspoon, scoop the pulp and seeds from the centre of each piece of cucumber. Pat dry with kitchen paper towels.
2 Drain the tuna fish and put it in a bowl. Add the butter, cheese, herbs and lemon juice, and mash well with a fork. Season to taste.
3 Stuff the cucumber pieces with the tuna fish mixture, and put in the refrigerator for at least 1 hour.
4 Before serving, cut each piece of cucumber into slices.

Potato Sticks

CUCUMBER RAITA SALAD

This cool Indian salad makes a marvellous accompaniment to hot, spicy dishes.

Serves 4

1 large cucumber, peeled
and thinly sliced
½ tsp salt
1¼ cups/300 ml unflavoured/natural
yogurt
3 tbs chopped fresh mint
freshly ground black
pepper

1 Put the cucumber slices into a sieve, sprinkle with salt, and leave to drain for 30 minutes.
2 Put the yogurt into a serving dish with half the mint. Add the cucumber, season with pepper, and stir well.
3 Chill until needed, and then garnish with the remaining mint.

POTATO RAITA

Serves 4

1 lb/450g potatoes, peeled and
boiled
½ lb/225g tomatoes, sliced
freshly ground black
pepper
salt
½ tsp cumin seeds
2 cups/500 ml unflavoured/natural
yogurt
2 tbs chopped fresh coriander
leaves

1 When the potatoes are cool, slice them and mix with the sliced tomatoes.
2 Mix a generous sprinkling of black pepper, a pinch of salt and the cumin seeds with the yogurt, and pour over the potato-tomato mixture.
3 Decorate with the chopped coriander.

CARROT CASSEROLE

Serves 4

2½ cups/400g carrots, sliced
1 small onion, peeled and
finely chopped
salt
freshly ground black
pepper
1 tbs honey
¼ cup/35g soy/soya grits
2 tbs chopped fresh dill
¼ cup/25g sunflower seeds
1 egg, lightly beaten
1 cup/50g almonds, chopped

1 Place the carrots, onion, ½ cup/125 ml water and some salt into a saucepan. Bring to the boil, cover and simmer until the carrots are barely tender.
2 Stir in all the remaining ingredients except for the almonds and pour into a shallow baking dish.

3 Sprinkle with the almonds and bake in a preheated oven at 350°F/180°C, Gas Mark 4 for 15 minutes.

LIMA BEANS WITH SAVORY

Serves 4

2 tbs corn oil
1 onion, peeled and finely
chopped
1 garlic clove, peeled and
crushed
1 tbs chopped fresh parsley
1 tbs chopped fresh savory
2 lb/900g lima/broad beans, shelled
2½ cups/600 ml vegetable stock
(see page 63)
salt
freshly grated nutmeg
1 cup/250 ml cultured sour cream

1 Heat the oil in a large pan and fry the onion and garlic gently until soft.
2 Add the parsley, savory, beans, stock, salt, pepper and nutmeg and simmer until tender – about 5–10 minutes, depending on the age of the beans.
3 Drain off the liquid (use it again as a soup base), and stir the cream into the beans. Sprinkle with parsley and serve.

MUSHROOM AND HERB CASSEROLE

Serves 4

2 tbs/25g butter
¼ lb/125g bacon, cut into pieces
1 garlic clove, peeled and
crushed
½ tsp each of chopped fresh
thyme, oregano, basil
and rosemary

$\frac{3}{4}$ **tsp** paprika
1$\frac{1}{2}$ **lb/700g** mushrooms
salt
freshly ground black
pepper
$\frac{3}{4}$ **cup/175 ml** tomato sauce, hot
home-made
$\frac{1}{4}$ **lb/125g** Parmesan cheese, grated

1 Preheat the oven to 375°F/190°C, Gas Mark 5.
2 Melt the butter in a wide, heavy, flameproof casserole dish. Add the bacon and fry, stirring, until the fat runs.
3 Add the garlic, herbs and paprika, reduce the heat, and cook for 2 minutes.
4 Add the mushrooms and cook for 3 minutes, stirring. Season well.
5 Pour the tomato sauce over the mushrooms. Sprinkle the cheese on top and cook on the top shelf of the oven for 10 minutes or until browned.

Carrot Casserole

TURNIPS BRAISED WITH BACON AND SAGE

Serves 4

$\frac{1}{4}$ **lb/125g** bacon, chopped
1 small onion, peeled and chopped
1$\frac{1}{2}$ **lb/700g** turnips, peeled
1$\frac{1}{4}$ **cups/300 ml** bone stock (see page 63)
1$\frac{1}{2}$ **tbs** chopped fresh sage
salt
freshly ground black
pepper

1 Put the bacon into a large saucepan and fry over low heat until the fat runs. Add the onion to the pan and fry for 3 minutes.
2 Cut the turnips into quarters, or sixths if they are large, and add them to the pan with the beef stock, sage, salt and pepper.
3 Cover the pan and bring to the boil. Reduce the heat and simmer for 15 minutes, or until the turnips are just tender. Transfer the turnips to a serving dish and keep warm.
4 Reduce the cooking liquor to a good $\frac{1}{4}$ cup/75 ml by boiling rapidly. Pour over the turnips and serve immediately.

PEAS WITH GRAPEFRUIT AND MINT

Serves 4

2 **lb/1.8 kg** fresh garden peas, shelled
2 grapefruit
1 small bunch of mint
salt
freshly ground black
pepper

1 Put the peas into a saucepan with the grated rind and juice of one of the grapefruit.
2 Cut the peel and pith from the other grapefruit. Working over the pan, cut the membrane away from the segments of fruit. Add the grapefruit segments to the peas along with 1$\frac{1}{2}$ tablespoons of the mint, chopped, and some salt and pepper.
3 Cover the pan and bring to the boil slowly. Reduce the heat and simmer gently for 15 minutes, or until the peas are just tender and almost all the juice has been absorbed.
4 Serve hot, garnished with sprigs of the remaining mint.

Rosemary

CAULIFLOWER WITH SORREL SAUCE

A sharp sorrel sauce containing no flour makes an unusual and interesting alternative to the cheese sauce normally served with cauliflower.

Serves 4

1 large cauliflower
Sauce
6 sorrel leaves
1 **tbs/15g** butter
2$\frac{1}{2}$ **tbs** dry white wine
1 **cup/250 ml** cream
salt
freshly ground black
pepper

1 Clean and prepare the cauliflower and break into neat florets. Steam until cooked but still firm.
2 Meanwhile make the sauce. De-stalk the sorrel leaves, chop finely and sweat in a little butter very briefly. Add the white wine and reduce. Stir in the cream, reduce again until the sauce is smooth and well blended, and season to taste. Do not boil or allow the sorrel and cream to stand for too long, otherwise the sauce may curdle. Coat the cauliflower with sauce and serve at once.

TABBOULI

Serves 6–8

1 cup/175g burghul (cracked wheat)
1 lettuce
2 cups/30g chopped fresh parsley
½ cup/8g shallots, peeled and chopped
½ cup/8g chopped fresh mint
juice of 1 lemon
1 tsp allspice or freshly ground black pepper
3 ripe tomatoes, peeled and finely chopped
¼ cup/65 ml olive oil
lemon wedges, to garnish

1 Soak the burghul in 2 cups of water for 20 minutes before preparing the salad.
2 Chop the lettuce leaves finely, leaving a few whole as a base for the salad. Put the shredded lettuce in a bowl.
3 Add the parsley, shallots, mint and lemon juice to the shredded lettuce, and season with allspice or pepper.
4 Dry the burghul and mix in with the tomatoes and olive oil.
5 Place the whole lettuce leaves on a platter, mount the mixture on top, and garnish with lemon wedges to serve.

PERSIAN RICE WITH HERBS

A delicious accompaniment to fish, this rice dish is traditionally served at New Year in Iran because its greenness is believed to ensure happiness in the year ahead. Any fresh herbs may be added.

Basil

Serves 4

½ lb/225g Basmati or long-grain rice
1½ tbs chopped fresh chives
1½ tbs chopped fresh parsley
2½ tbs chopped mixed fresh herbs (tarragon, thyme, marjoram, basil)
grated rind of ½ lemon
salt
freshly ground black pepper

1 Put the rice into a saucepan and cover with 2½ cups/625 ml water. Bring to the boil, lower the heat and simmer for 5 minutes.
2 Add the herbs to the rice, stir in the lemon rind, and season with salt and pepper.
3 Mix well, cover the pan, and simmer gently for 10 minutes, or until the rice is tender and the water has been absorbed.

EGGPLANT À LA NÎMOISE

Serves 2

3½ tbs olive oil
1 large eggplant/aubergine, halved, degorged, rinsed and dried
¼ lb/125g cooked rice
3 tomatoes, peeled, seeded and chopped
1 tbs tomato paste/purée
1 garlic clove, peeled and crushed
1½ tbs chopped fresh basil
1 tsp chopped fresh chives
salt
freshly ground black pepper

1 Preheat the oven to 350°F/180°C, Gas Mark 4.
2 Heat the oil in a skillet and add the eggplant/aubergine, skin side uppermost. Reduce the heat to low, cover the pan, and cook for about 10 minutes. Remove the eggplant/aubergine halves from the pan and drain them well.
3 Scoop out the pulp with a teaspoon, leaving the skin intact.
4 Chop the pulp and mix with the rice, tomatoes, tomato paste/purée, garlic, basil and chives. Season with salt and pepper to taste.
5 Fill the skins with the stuffing and place them in a baking dish. Sprinkle with a little oil from the skillet and bake for about 35 minutes. Serve at once.

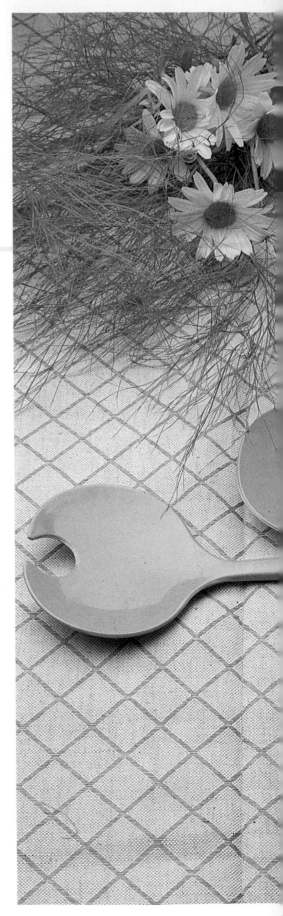

DANDELION GREENS WITH BACON

For a dandelion salad instead of a hot vegetable dish, choose the youngest and most tender of leaves, and serve them raw, dressed with the fat from the bacon, a garlic French dressing, the bacon and a few garlic croûtons, if liked.

Serves 4

¼ lb/125g bacon, chopped
½ lb/225g dandelion leaves, washed
salt
freshly ground black pepper

1 Put the bacon into a saucepan and fry gently over low heat until the fat runs.
2 Add the dandelion leaves to the bacon, and fry, stirring constantly, for 1 minute.
3 Add a good ¼ cup/75 ml water, salt and pepper. Cover the pan and cook over low heat for about 2 minutes, or until the leaves are tender but still a bright green colour. Serve hot.

LEMON AND HERB CAULIFLOWER

Serves 4

1 medium to large cauliflower
1½ **tbs** lemon juice
salt
freshly ground black pepper
1½ **tbs** chopped fresh parsley
1½ **tbs** chopped fresh chives

1 Remove and coarsely chop the leaves of the cauliflower. Divide the cauliflower into florets.
2 Put the florets and the chopped leaves into a large pan. Pour in ⅔ cup/150 ml boiling water and the lemon juice. Sprinkle with salt and pepper.
3 Cover the pan and simmer over low heat for 5–8 minutes, or until the cauliflower is tender but still crisp.
4 Remove the cauliflower to a warm serving dish and keep hot. Boil the cooking liquor rapidly for 2 minutes, or until it is reduced to just over 4 tablespoons.
5 Stir in the chopped herbs, and pour the green liquor over the cauliflower. Serve immediately.

Tabbouli

Thyme

A GLORIOUS SALAD

From a notebook of Kentish recipes dated 1841, this outstanding salad is a perfect starting course for an early summer dinner. It was intended to be served on a large flat dish with a wreath of nasturtium flowers around it, but is better served in individual dishes with thin slices of brown bread and butter.

Serves 6

6 artichoke hearts, or a can of smaller ones, well drained
24 tiny new potatoes, boiled, cooled and cut in half
1 lettuce heart, very finely shredded
1 tbs finely chopped fresh parsley
1 tsp each of finely chopped fresh tarragon, mint and thyme
¼ lb/125g very young green/French beans, boiled and cut in half
12 very young carrots, scraped, boiled and finely sliced
⅔ cup/150 ml salad dressing (see page 65)
12 nasturtium flowers

1 In each of six dishes first put the artichokes, cut in halves or quarters, according to size, and the potatoes, then a layer of chopped lettuce.
2 Mix all the herbs together and sprinkle about half on the lettuce.
3 Pile the green/French beans and carrots on this, pour over the dressing, and sprinkle with the rest of the herbs.
4 Finally, put two nasturtium flowers on each dish.

POTATOES BRAISED IN RED WINE

Serves 4

1½ lb/700g potatoes, peeled
1¼ cups/300 ml dry red wine
2½ tbs chopped fresh thyme
2½ tbs chopped fresh parsley
salt
freshly ground black pepper

1 Preheat the oven to 375°F/190°C, Gas Mark 5. Cut the potatoes into ¼in/6mm slices.
2 Put the potatoes into a casserole or ovenproof dish and pour in the dry red wine.
3 Sprinkle with the thyme, parsley, salt and pepper. Mix lightly so that all the potatoes are coated with wine and herbs.
4 Cover and bake for about 1 hour, or until the potatoes are tender and almost all the wine has been absorbed. The potatoes will be a delicate pink colour on the outside, but still white inside. Serve hot.

HERB BAKED NEW POTATOES

Serves 4

1½ lb/700g new potatoes, scrubbed
salt
freshly ground black pepper
1 small bunch of fresh mint
1 small bunch of fresh parsley

1 Preheat the oven to 400°F/200°C, Gas Mark 6 and grease a sheet of foil large enough to enclose the potatoes.
2 Put the potatoes into the centre of the foil and sprinkle them with salt and pepper. Put 4 mint sprigs and 4 parsley sprigs among the potatoes. Fold the foil around them and seal the edges.
3 Bake the foil bag for 30–45 minutes, depending on the size of the potatoes, or until they are tender.
4 Remove the potatoes from the foil and put them in a serving dish. Sprinkle them with the remaining herbs, finely chopped.

STUFFED PEPPERS

A rich stuffing, varied in flavour and texture, baked in crisp green peppers, makes a tasty dish for lunch or supper.

Serves 4

6 oz/175g brown rice
4 medium tomatoes, blanched, peeled, halved and seeded
¼ lb/125g cooked peeled shrimp/prawns
1 large onion, peeled and finely chopped
2 oz/50g anchovy fillets, chopped
1 garlic clove, peeled and crushed
1½ tbs chopped fresh parsley
1½ tbs chopped fresh thyme
8 stuffed olives, sliced
salt
freshly ground black pepper
4 green peppers
good ¼ cup/75 ml chicken stock (see page 64)

1 Preheat the oven to 375°F/190°C, Gas Mark 5.
2 First prepare the filling. Cook the brown rice in 1¼ cups/300 ml water for 30 minutes, or until the rice is tender and the water has been absorbed.
3 Chop the tomatoes and put them into a mixing bowl with the cooked rice.
4 Add the shrimp/prawns, the onion, anchovy fillets and garlic and combine with the herbs, olives, salt and pepper. Mix thoroughly.
5 Cut a slice off the top of the peppers, and remove the white pith and seeds. Stand the peppers upright, cutting a small slice off the bottom if necessary, in an ovenproof dish or small roasting pan. Divide the filling among them.
6 Pour the chicken stock into the dish, and cover the dish with foil. Bake for 30–40 minutes, or until the peppers are tender. Serve hot or cold.

Stuffed Peppers

MUSHROOMS POACHED WITH LEMON AND HERBS

Serves 4

> 1 lb/450g mushrooms, washed and
>   stalks trimmed
> 1 lemon, rind and juice
>   salt
>   freshly ground black
>   pepper
> 4 fresh thyme sprigs
> 1 large parsley sprig

1 Cut large mushrooms into halves or quarters, and leave small ones whole.
2 Put the mushrooms into a pan with the rind and juice of the lemon, the salt, pepper, and herbs.
3 Cover the pan and cook over very low heat for about 2 minutes, or until the mushrooms are tender (overcooking will toughen them).
4 Serve hot or cold.

FENNEL BRAISED WITH APPLE

Serves 4

> 2 large fennel bulbs,
>   washed
> 1 large cooking apple,
>   peeled and cored
> $\frac{2}{3}$ **cup/150 ml** chicken stock
>   (see page 64)
> 1$\frac{1}{2}$ **tbs** lemon juice
>   salt
>   freshly ground black
>   pepper
> $\frac{1}{2}$ **tbs** chopped fresh fennel (or
>   the leaves from the top
>   of the bulb)
> $\frac{1}{2}$ **tbs** chopped fresh parsley

1 Preheat the oven to 350°F/180°C, Gas Mark 4.
2 Cut the fennel bulbs into quarters lengthways, and put the pieces into a casserole or ovenproof dish.
3 Cut the apple into slices and put them into the casserole with the chicken stock, lemon juice, salt and pepper to taste.
4 Cover and bake for 30 minutes, or until the fennel is tender but not soft.
5 Drain the stock into a saucepan and boil for about 3 minutes, or until it is reduced to about 4 tablespoons. Pour the sauce over the fennel, sprinkle with the herbs, and serve immediately.

Fennel Braised with Apple

AVOCADO AND ORANGE MINT SALAD

Serves 4

> 2 ripe avocado pears,
>   peeled
> 2 oranges, peeled and
>   segmented
> $\frac{2}{3}$ **cup/150 ml** unflavoured/natural
>   yogurt
> 2$\frac{1}{2}$ **tbs** chopped fresh mint
> 4 mint sprigs, to garnish

1 Slice the avocados, and arrange on a plate alternately with the orange segments.
2 Mix together the yogurt and chopped mint, pour over the salad, and garnish with whole mint sprigs.

POLE BEANS WITH GARLIC AND SAGE

Serves 4

> 1 lb/450g pole/runner beans,
>   topped and tailed
> 1$\frac{1}{2}$ **tbs** corn oil
> 2 garlic cloves, peeled and
>   crushed
> 1$\frac{1}{2}$ **tbs** chopped fresh sage
>   salt
>   freshly ground black
>   pepper
> 1$\frac{1}{2}$ **tbs** chopped fresh parsley

1 String the beans as well, if necessary, and cut them into diagonal slices about 1in/2.5cm long.
2 Heat the oil in a saucepan and add the

garlic. Fry gently for 1 minute, or until lightly browned.

3 Stir in the chopped sage, followed by the beans, $\frac{2}{3}$ cup/150 ml water, and salt and pepper.

4 Cover the pan and bring to the boil. Reduce the heat and simmer for about 5 minutes, or until the beans are tender, but still slightly crisp.

5 Serve hot or cold, sprinkled with the chopped parsley.

FRENCH PEAS

This French method of cooking peas with lettuce, mint and scallions/spring onions is delicious.

Serves 4–6

> 1 round lettuce
> 2 lb/900g fresh garden peas, shelled
> 4 scallions/spring onions, chopped
> 1 small bunch of mint
>   salt
>   freshly ground black pepper

1 Wash but do not drain the leaves of the lettuce. Put the larger outside leaves into a saucepan.

2 Put the peas on top of the lettuce and top them with the scallions/spring onions, 1 tablespoon of chopped mint, and salt and pepper. Shred the remaining lettuce and put it on top of the peas. Add $4\frac{1}{2}$ tablespoons of water.

3 Cover the pan, bring slowly to the boil, then reduce the heat and simmer gently for 15 minutes, or until the peas are tender.

4 Transfer to a serving dish, with the cooking liquid, garnish with sprigs of mint, and serve.

CHICK-PEAS A LA GRECQUE

Serves 4

> $\frac{1}{4}$ **lb/125g** chick-peas
> $1\frac{1}{2}$ **tbs** olive oil
> **2** small onions, peeled and finely sliced
> $\frac{1}{4}$ **lb/125g** button mushrooms
> $2\frac{1}{2}$ **cups/625 ml** white wine
> **2 tsp** tomato paste/purée
> **1 tsp** chopped fresh oregano (or $\frac{1}{2}$ tsp dried)
> **1** bay leaf
>   salt
>   freshly ground black pepper

1 Soak the chick-peas overnight in cold water.

2 Simmer for about $1\frac{1}{2}$ hours in fresh water to cover, until almost cooked. Drain well.

3 Heat the oil in a pan and fry the onions gently until transparent. Add the button mushrooms and chick-peas, then pour over the wine. Add the tomato paste/purée, herbs and seasoning.

4 Heat to boiling point, then simmer for 30 minutes. Leave to cool and serve chilled.

Bay

ZUCCHINI WITH LEMON AND HERBS

Serves 4

$1\frac{1}{2}$ lb/700g zucchini/courgettes,
washed
$\frac{1}{2}$ lemon, rind and juice
$1\frac{1}{2}$ **tbs** chopped fresh parsley
$1\frac{1}{2}$ **tbs** chopped fresh thyme
salt
freshly ground black
pepper
good $\frac{1}{4}$ **cup/75 ml** chicken or vegetable
stock (see page 63)

1 Thickly slice the zucchini/courgettes. Preheat the oven to 350°F/180°C, Gas Mark 4.
2 In a small bowl mix together the grated lemon rind, herbs, salt and pepper.
3 Arrange the zucchini/courgette slices in an ovenproof dish, sprinkling each layer with the herb mixture.
4 Squeeze the juice of the lemon into a small bowl and add the stock. Pour the liquid over the zucchini/courgettes.
5 Cover and bake for 30 minutes, until the zucchini/courgettes are just tender but not soft. Alternatively, put all the ingredients into a saucepan and cook, covered, for 10 minutes, or until the zucchini/courgettes are tender.

GREEN BEANS WITH TARRAGON

The combination of two kinds of beans – one whole, the other puréed – gives this dish a special character.

Serves 4

1 lb/450g young lima/broad beans,
podded
1 potato, peeled and
chopped
2 onions, peeled
1 garlic clove, peeled and
chopped
1 **tbs/15g** butter
salt
freshly ground black
pepper
$1\frac{1}{2}$ **tbs** chopped fresh tarragon
a squeeze of lemon juice
$\frac{1}{2}$ **lb/225g** young green/French
beans, topped and
tailed

1 Chop the whole lima/broad beans coarsely and cook gently in water with the chopped potato and one of the onions, chopped. When the potato is soft, pass the combined mixture through a sieve.
2 Chop the other onion and mix with the garlic. Cook gently in the butter in a pan. Stir in the lima/broad bean purée and adjust the consistency by adding water and more butter if necessary.
3 Season to taste and toss in the tarragon. Finish with a squeeze of lemon juice and keep warm.
4 Cook the green/French beans briefly in a little salted water until just cooked but still crisp, then drain.
5 To serve, spread some of the sauce onto warm plates, and place the French beans on top.

FATTOUSH

This is a "peasant salad" from the Lebanon.

Serves 4

1 round of Lebanese bread
(or pitta), toasted
2 cucumbers, peeled and
sliced
$\frac{1}{2}$ lettuce, washed and
shredded
2 shallots, peeled and
chopped
$\frac{1}{2}$ **cup/8g** each of chopped fresh
parsley and mint
juice of 1 lemon
$\frac{1}{2}$ **cup/125ml** olive oil
2 garlic cloves, peeled and
crushed
salt
freshly ground black
pepper
red sweet pepper or
cucumber, for garnish

1 Cut the bread into cubes and sprinkle with a little water. Place in a bowl with the cucumber, lettuce, shallots, parsley and mint, and toss them together until well mixed.
2 Place lemon juice, oil, garlic, salt and pepper in a jar and shake well.
3 Pour the dressing over the salad, garnish with shredded red pepper or very thinly sliced unpeeled cucumber, and serve.

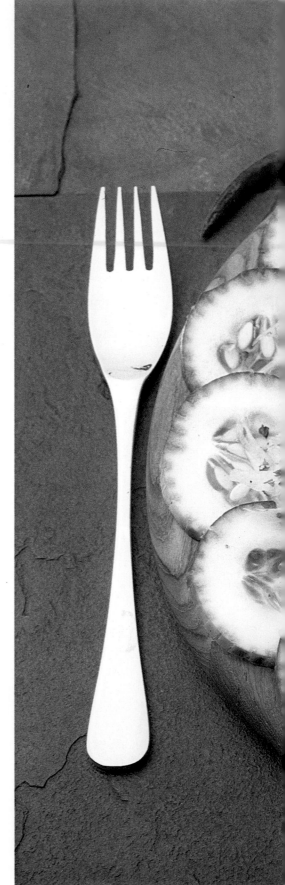

Fattoush

DESSERTS AND BAKING

Most herbs are associated with savoury cooking, but a few can be used successfully in puddings or desserts, especially those composed of fruit. Sweet cicely is the "sugar-saver" herb, and, if used with sourer fruits – in stewed fruit dishes, or in compotes, mousses and fruit salads – it adds its own sweet flavour and character. Angelica, too, raw and cooked, can be added to fruit dishes – and, of course, preserved and candied (see page 109), it decorates trifles, cakes and many cold desserts. Mint too can be used successfully in and on sweets, sherbets/sorbets benefitting particularly from its cool flavour. Rose hips and elderflowers lend themselves to particular sweet uses; and elderflower florets and leaves such as borage can be dipped into a batter and then deep-fried as sweet fritters. Many herbs can add their fragrance to creams and to batters, and can flavour sugars for baking in the same way as vanilla. Bay leaves add a wonderful tang when baked with a custard or rice pudding, and rose geranium leaves can be placed in the bottom of a pan used for baking a sponge cake.

Use herbs in non-sweet baking as well. Your favourite home-made bread recipe can be transformed by the subtle flavours of added herbs (it is easy to overdo it, though, so start with a pinch only). Sprinkle herb seeds like fennel or dill on top of bread before it is baked, or use a herb butter to spread between the slices of a bought French loaf for a herb-garlic bread.

ROSE HIP SOUP

This Scandinavian fruit soup is really a purée of rose hips that can be served as a sweet.

Serves 4

1 lb/450g rose hips, trimmed and washed
2 tbs arrowroot
honey
1 oz/25g flaked almonds

1 Put the rose hips in a saucepan with $2\frac{1}{2}$ cups/625 ml water. Cover the pan and bring to the boil. Reduce the heat and simmer for 20–30 minutes, or until the rose hips are tender.
2 Liquidize the rose hips with the water and then sieve the purée into a saucepan.
3 Blend the arrowroot with a little of the purée, then stir into the fruit purée in the pan. Bring to the boil, stirring constantly, and boil until the soup thickens.
4 Sweeten to taste with a little honey and simmer for 2 minutes more.
5 Pour into four individual serving dishes or one large dish and leave to cool. Serve chilled, sprinkled with the flaked almonds.

STEWED FRUIT WITH SWEET CICELY

$1\frac{1}{2}$ lb/700g fruit, prepared and chopped if necessary
a handful of sweet cicely stems and leaves, chopped
sugar to taste

1 Put the fruit into a heavy pan with the sweet cicely and cover with water.
2 Cook very slowly until the fruit is soft. Taste for sweetness, and add sugar to taste.
3 Serve as it is, or sieve for a smoother purée. Serve with whipped cream.

MARIGOLD PUDDING

The earliest recipes for this pudding occur in 14th-century manuscripts. This one comes from Arundel in Sussex. Flowers were used in cooking for their colour and flavour in the Middle Ages as a matter of course. Rose petals, violets, borage, cowslips and marigolds were all used as an integral part of various creams and tarts. Nasturtium flowers and striped carnation petals were used for decoration on salads and cold creams. Serve the gloriously orange Marigold Pudding (which is lighter than the usual flour and suet pudding) very hot, with plenty of thick cream. The marigolds give it a very subtle flavour.

$2\frac{1}{2}$ cups/25g marigold petals, chopped (reserving a few whole for decoration)
1 cup/120g shredded suet
4 tbs clear honey
$\frac{1}{4}$ cup/60g sugar
the crust from a large crusty white loaf of bread, finely grated (about $1\frac{1}{2}$ cups/240g)
$\frac{2}{3}$–$1\frac{1}{4}$ cups/ 150–300 ml milk

1 Mix all the ingredients except for the milk well together, then stir in only just enough milk to bind.
2 Put the pudding in a well buttered bowl and cover closely with foil.
3 Stand the bowl in a saucepan of boiling water (the water must come about halfway up the sides of the bowl) and steam for 3 hours. Never let the water go off the boil. Fill up with boiling water from time to time.
4 Turn out and sprinkle the reserved marigold petals on top.

ELDERFLOWER PANCAKES

Exquisitely perfumed elderflowers lift pancakes into the realms of the exotic.

Makes about 8 pancakes

¼ lb/125g flour
a small pinch of salt
1 egg
1¼ cups/300 ml milk
12 elderflower clusters
melted butter
sugar

1 Sift the flour and salt into a bowl. Make a well in the centre and drop in the egg and half the milk. Beat well until frothy then stir in the rest of the milk.
2 Wash the elderflowers thoroughly in salted water. Pick off the little heads and fold them into the batter.
3 Put just enough melted butter into an iron or non-stick skillet to coat the bottom, and make the pancakes in the usual way.
4 Serve hot with a dusting of sugar.

HERB RYE CRISPBREAD

Makes 18 crispbreads

½ lb/225g rye flour
4 tbs/50g margarine
1 tsp dried mixed herbs
½ tsp salt
5 tbs milk or water

1 Preheat the oven to 400°F/200°C, Gas Mark 6.
2 Put the rye flour into a mixing bowl and rub in the margarine.
3 Mix in the dried mixed herbs and salt, then gradually add the milk or water. Mix until the ingredients are thoroughly blended and the dough is firm.
4 Divide the dough into halves. Knead each half lightly on a floured surface. Roll each piece of dough out thinly to about 9in/22.5cm square. Cut into 3in/7.5cm squares.
5 Put the squares onto lightly greased baking sheets, and prick each square well to prevent it from rising and bubbling during baking.
6 Bake the crispbreads for 10–15 minutes, or until the edges just begin to colour, but do not let them brown. Cool them slightly on the baking sheets, then transfer them to wire racks.

GARLIC HERB FRENCH BREAD

Makes 2 French sticks

1½ lb/700g all-purpose/plain flour
salt
½ oz/15g fresh yeast
2 cups/500 ml tepid water
½ cup/125g butter
3–4 garlic cloves, peeled and finely chopped
1½ tbs dried mixed herbs
1½ tbs chopped fresh parsley

1 Put the flour into a large mixing bowl with 1 tablespoon salt.
2 Blend the yeast with the tepid water until the yeast has dissolved.
3 Make a well in the flour and pour in the yeast liquid. Mix the ingredients together to form a firm dough.
4 Turn the dough out onto a floured surface and knead it well for 10 minutes, or until the dough becomes firm and elastic and is no longer sticky.
5 Lightly grease a large bowl. Put the dough into the bowl and cover with greased plastic wrap/polythene. Leave the dough to rise in a warm place for 45–60 minutes, or until it has doubled in bulk.
6 Meanwhile soften the butter in a bowl. Add the garlic and the herbs and mix well.
7 When the dough has risen, turn it out onto a floured surface and knead it again for 2–3 minutes.
8 Divide it in two and roll each half out to form an oval as long as a baking sheet, about 14 × 10in/35 × 25cm.
9 Spread half of the prepared butter mixture on each piece of dough, leaving a 1in/2.5cm margin all around the edges. Roll each oval up tightly lengthways and seal the edges.
10 Place the loaves with the seams underneath on a well greased baking sheet. Make diagonal slits into the tops of the loaves at 2in/5cm intervals. Cover the baking sheet with greased plastic wrap/polythene and leave the dough to rise in a warm place for 20–30 minutes. Preheat the oven to 425°F/220°C, Gas Mark 7.
11 Remove the polythene from the loaves. For a crisp crust, brush the loaves with 1 teaspoon salt dissolved in 5 tablespoons water.
12 Bake the loaves for 15 minutes, or until they are crisp and golden brown. Remove the loaves from the oven and

tap the base of each. If they sound hollow the bread is ready.
13 Serve immediately, or leave to cool on a wire rack.

SAVOURY COUNTRY LOAF

¾ lb/350g strong white all-purpose/plain flour
¾ lb/350g whole wheat flour
1½ tbs salt
freshly ground black pepper
¼ lb/125g strong Cheddar cheese, grated
¼ lb/125g bacon, chopped and grilled
1½ tbs chopped fresh sage
½ oz/15g fresh yeast
2 cups/500 ml tepid water

1 In a large bowl mix together the flours, the salt and a pinch of pepper.
2 Mix in 3 oz/75 g of the grated cheese along with the bacon and sage.
3 Blend the yeast with the tepid water until the yeast has dissolved.
4 Make a well in the dry ingredients and pour in the yeast liquid. Mix the ingredients together to a firm dough.
5 Turn the dough out onto a lightly floured surface and knead it well for 10 minutes, or until it is firm and elastic and is no longer sticky.
6 Put the dough into a lightly greased bowl and cover with greased plastic wrap/polythene. Leave the dough to rise in a warm place for 45–60 minutes, or until it has doubled in bulk.
7 When the dough has risen, turn it out onto a lightly floured surface and knead it for 2–3 minutes.
8 Cut a quarter off the dough. Shape the larger piece into a ball and place on a greased baking sheet. Shape the smaller piece of dough into a ball and place it on top of the larger ball. Flour the handle of a wooden spoon and push it through the centre of both balls, then pull it out again quickly.
9 Cover the baking sheet with greased plastic wrap/polythene and leave the dough to rise in a warm place for 20–30 minutes, or until it has doubled in bulk. Preheat the oven to 425°F/220°C, Gas Mark 7.
10 Sprinkle the loaf with the remaining grated cheese. Bake the loaf for 30 minutes or until it is well risen, browned and sounds hollow when tapped underneath. Cool on a wire rack.

DRINKS AND PRESERVES

Apart from the refreshing and health-giving teas and tisanes discussed on page 20, some herbs are most associated with drinks – the enlivening borage, the cucumber-flavoured salad burnet, and sweet woodruff. Any wine may simply be steeped with a herb for additional flavour – the three above, or elderflowers, lavender, lemon balm or verbena, mint or rosemary. Elderflowers make a refreshing drink in themselves, and rose hips can be made into a syrup which is rich in vitamin C. Mint is one of the most useful herbs and plays a major part in classic mint juleps, as a garnish on many other cocktails, and makes one of the most refreshing teas, whether hot or cold. But try yogurt drinks with herbs, fruit juices with herbs – tomato with basil or chervil, for instance – and mixed infusions.

Herbs may be preserved in a number of ways – dried, frozen, immersed in oil, or made into vinegars and oils (see pages 22 and 23) – but they can also lend their flavours to herb jellies and pickles. Candying and crystallizing are less long-lasting methods of preservation, but can bring the freshness and colour of herb flowers and leaves to many branches of cookery.

WOODRUFF CUP

When woodruff is dried, it has a much fuller flavour and is more aromatic.

Makes 12–15 glasses

> 2 **bottles** dry white wine
> 3–4 sprigs of dried woodruff
> 1 lemon, rind and juice
> $\frac{1}{2}$ **lb/225g** soft fruit (strawberries, raspberries etc)
> sugar to taste
> 2 **bottles** soda water, or to taste
> borage or mint leaves

1 Put half of one bottle of wine into a large punch bowl with the woodruff and leave to stand for 30–60 minutes.
2 Filter or strain, discarding the woodruff, and then add the remaining ingredients, decorating the top with the borage or mint leaves.

ELDERFLOWER WATER

Elderflowers make a refreshing summer drink that may be stored in a cool place for several weeks.

Makes 6 cups/1.5 litres

> 2$\frac{1}{2}$ **cups/625 ml** elderflowers
> 2 lemons, rind and juice
> $\frac{1}{2}$ **lb/225g** sugar

1 Cut enough elderflower florets to give about 2$\frac{1}{2}$ cups/625 ml of tightly packed flowers.
2 Put them into a large bowl with the rind and juice of the lemons and the sugar.
3 Pour in 6 cups/1.5 litres of boiling water and stir until the sugar has dissolved.
4 Cover the bowl and leave to stand overnight. Strain the liquid and pour it into bottles. Serve chilled.

MINT JULEP

Purists swear that juleps should be made in silver mugs and with bourbon. The ice must be crushed very finely and dried as thoroughly as possible – and the mug or glass must be thoroughly chilled.

Per glass

> 9 fresh mint sprigs
> 1 **tsp** sugar
> crushed ice
> bourbon (or Scotch whisky)

1 Put 6 mint sprigs into an iced mug or tall glass.
2 Pour in the sugar and crush the mint into the sugar.
3 Add the crushed ice, then pour in the bourbon. Stir gently.
4 Pack in more ice, stir, and then garnish with the remaining mint sprigs. Wipe the glass and serve.

RED WINE CUP

Makes about 15 glasses

> 2 **bottles** red wine
> 2 **tbs** sugar
> 4 **tbs** hot water
> $\frac{1}{2}$ lemon, rind and juice
> 1 **tsp** grated nutmeg
> 10 lemon verbena leaves
> 2 **bottles** soda water, or to taste
> 5 fresh borage sprigs

1 Pour the red wine into a large jug or bowl.
2 Dissolve the sugar in the hot water.
3 Mix the water with the wine, and add all the other ingredients except for the borage.
4 Leave to stand for about 30 minutes, then strain into a large punch bowl. Decorate with the borage.

Mint

ROSE HIP SYRUP

Rose hips were used in medieval times as a filling for tarts. During World War II they were highly valued for their vitamin C content.

1 lb/450g rose hips, washed,
trimmed and ground/
minced
½ lb/225g sugar

1 Bring 5 cups/1 litre of water to the boil in a saucepan. Put in the ground/minced hips and bring back to the boil. Immediately draw the pan off the heat and leave for 20 minutes.
2 Pour the contents of the pan through a scalded jelly bag. When it stops dripping, return the pulp to the pan.
3 Pour in a scant 2 cups/450 ml of water and bring to the boil. As soon as it boils, draw the pan off the heat and leave for 10 minutes. Pour through the jelly bag.
4 When the dripping has stopped, pour all the juice into a clean pan and bring to the boil. Boil briskly until the liquid measures about 2 cups/500 ml.
5 Reduce the heat and stir in the sugar. When dissolved, boil for 5 minutes.
6 Pour the syrup into clean bottles. If you make large quantities, then you will have to seal and sterilize the bottles. A small quantity only can be safely kept in the refrigerator for a week or two.

PICKLED NASTURTIUM SEEDS

These make an excellent substitute for capers. The nasturtium seeds must be picked as soon as the flowers fade and before they become hard.

2½ cups/625 ml wine or cider vinegar
1 oz/25g salt
10 peppercorns
a few shreds of mace
a few gratings of peeled
horseradish
1 small onion, peeled and
chopped
1 bay leaf
nasturtium seeds

1 Put the vinegar into a saucepan and add the salt, peppercorns, mace, horseradish, chopped onion and the bay leaf. Bring to the boil and simmer for 5 minutes.
2 Pour the vinegar into a bowl, cover and allow to cool. When quite cold, strain the vinegar into a jar.

3 Pick the nasturtium seeds as the flowers fall and drop them into the spiced vinegar. Keep the jar tightly covered in a cool place. Leave for at least 30 days before eating the "capers".

CANDIED ANGELICA

Sweet cicely roots, peeled and sliced, can be candied similarly. Add some lemon juice to the sugar syrup.

young angelica stems and
thick leaf ribs
sugar

1 Pick the angelica in spring or early summer, before the plant flowers. Chop into pieces 2in/5cm long.
2 Put angelica into a pan and cover with water. Bring to the boil and simmer for about 5–10 minutes until tender. Lift out and scrape off the outer skin.
3 Return them to the water in the pan and simmer for a few more minutes until they turn bright green. Lift out, drain thoroughly and weigh.
4 Using the same weight of sugar as angelica, put the sugar into a pan with water (⅔ cup/150 ml water to each 1 lb/450 g sugar), and heat until the sugar dissolves. Boil to a thick syrup.
5 Put the angelica into the syrup and simmer until the stems are soft and transparent.
6 Leave the stems in the syrup – covered and in a cool place – for 2 weeks.
7 Drain well, coat with sugar and dry very thoroughly in a very low oven or, well protected, in an airy place, before storing in an airtight can or jar, between layers of wax/greaseproof paper.

HERB JELLIES

These are all made with a basis of apples, and many herbs can be added – mint, rosemary, thyme, sage, tarragon, bergamot, geranium leaves, lemon balm.

4 lb/1.8 kg cooking apples, washed
and chopped
1 large bunch of the chosen
herb
wine vinegar (for jellies
made from mint,
thyme, sage or
rosemary)
white sugar

1 Put the apples in a large preserving pan, and add the herb and water to cover. (Add half vinegar, half water to

mint, thyme, sage and rosemary jellies.)
2 Simmer until the apples are soft and pulpy then pour into a clean jelly bag suspended over a large bowl. Leave to drip overnight. Do not squeeze or press, or the jelly will be cloudy.
3 Measure the juice obtained, and for every 2½ cups/625 ml, add ¾ lb/350 g sugar.
4 Stir over a low heat until the sugar has dissolved and then boil until setting point is reached. Test for this by putting a teaspoonful of juice on a very cold saucer; push with your finger and if a skin wrinkles, the jelly is ready.
5 Leave for 10 minutes to cool slightly, then pour into warm clean jars. If you like, you could stir in some of the chopped leaf – mint is the most suitable for this – or float a whole leaf in each jar – sage, bergamot or lemon balm.

CANDIED FLOWERS AND LEAVES

Among the flowers, use violets, rose petals, nasturtiums, pelargoniums, bergamot and borage; use the leaves of mint, violet, pelargonium and lemon balm.

leaves and flowers
1 egg white
castor sugar

1 Gather the leaves and flowers on a sunny morning after the dew has evaporated, for they must be dry.
2 Put the egg white onto a saucer and beat lightly so that it turns opaque.
3 Using a pair of tweezers, dip each leaf or flower first into the egg white to coat thoroughly, and then into the sugar. Sprinkle the sugar gently and thoroughly over the flowers.
4 Shake off surplus sugar, then lay the flowers and leaves in a single layer on wax/greaseproof paper on a wire rack, and cover with another sheet.
5 Dry in a warm airy place or in a very low oven (with the door propped open) until completely dry and brittle. Store in single layers in airtight cans or boxes between layers of wax/greaseproof paper, for a day or two only.

INDEX

A

aches/pains: treatment for 26
Angelica 62
  in cosmetics 27
  cultivation 13, 17, 31
  harvesting 18
  identifying 31
  in medicine 26, 31
  preserving 19
  propagation 15

B

Balm: in cosmetics 27
  identifying 32
  in medicine 32
  oil 23
  see also Lemon balm
Basil 62
  cultivation 16, 17, 33
  harvesting 18
  identifying 33
  in medicine 26, 33
  oil 22
  preserving 19
  tea/tisane 20
  vinegar 23
baths, herbs for 27
Bay 6
  cultivation 14, 15, 16, 17, 34
  identifying 34
  in medicine 26, 34
  oil 23
  preserving 19
  propagation 15
  vinegar 23
Bergamot 10, 11
  cultivation 14
  identifying 59
  in medicine 26
  preserving 19
  propagation 15
  tea/tisane 21
Borage 9
  in cosmetics 29
  cultivation 14, 17, 35
  harvesting 18
  identifying 35
  in medicine 26, 35
  preserving 19
  propagation 15
  vinegar 23
Bowles mint: identifying 47
bruises: treatment for 26

C

catarrh: treatment for 26
Celery: harvesting 18
  identifying 59
  preserving 19
Chamomile: in compost 14
  in cosmetics 27, 29
  cultivation 14, 17
  harvesting 18
  identifying 59

  in medicine 26
  propagation 15
  tea/tisane 17, 21
  vinegar 23
Chervil: cultivation 13, 17, 36
  harvesting 18
  identifying 36
  in medicine 26, 36
  preserving 19
  propagation 15
  vinegar 23
chest troubles: treatments for 26
Chives 6
  cultivation 13, 17, 37
  identifying 37
  in medicine 26, 37
  preserving 19
  propagation 15
  vinegar 23
cleansers/lotions 29
colds: treatments for 26
Coltsfoot: in cosmetics 29
  identifying 59
  in medicine 26
Comfrey: in compost 14
  in cosmetics 27, 29
  cultivation 15, 17
  identifying 59
  propagation 15
  in medicine 26
compresses 26
constipation: treatments for 26
Coriander 8, 9
  in cosmetics 29
  cultivation 17, 38
  harvesting 18
  identifying 38
  in medicine 26, 38
  preserving 19
  propagation 15
  oil 22, 23
Corn mint: identifying 47
coughs: treatment for 26
cuts: treatment for 26

D

Dandelion: in compost 14
  in cosmetics 27, 29
  cultivation 17
  identifying 59
  in medicine 26
decoctions 24
digestion: treatments for 26
Dill: cultivation 14, 17, 38
  harvesting 18
  identifying 39
  in medicine 26, 38
  preserving 19
  propagation 15
  vinegar 23
Dock: in medicine 26

E

Eau de Cologne mint:

  identifying 47
Elder: cultivation 17
  harvesting 18
  identifying 59
  in medicine 26
Elderflower: in cosmetics 27, 29
  in medicine 26
  preserving 19
  vinegar 23
Evening primrose: medicine 24
eye bath 29
Eyebright: in cosmetics 29
  harvesting 18
  identifying 60
  in medicine 26

F

face packs/masks 27, 29
Fat-hen 8
Fennel 9, 62
  in cosmetics 27, 29
  cultivation 13, 14, 17, 40
  harvesting 18
  identifying 40
  in medicine 26, 40
  oil 22
  preserving 19
  propagation 15
  vinegar 23
Feverfew: cultivation 14
  harvesting 18
  identifying 60
  in medicine 24, 26
fevers: treatments for 26
flatulence: treatments for 26
Foxglove: in medicine 24

G

Garlic 7, 8
  cultivation 15, 17
  identifying 60
  in medicine 26
  vinegar 23
Geranium: in cosmetics 29
  identifying 60
  preserving 19
  see also Pelargonium
Ginseng: tea/tisane 21

H

hair rinses/conditioners 29
Hamburg parsley: cultivation
  17, 41
  harvesting 18, 41
  in medicine 41
headaches: treatment for 26
Horse mint: identifying 47
Horseradish: cultivation 14, 15,
  17, 42
  harvesting 18
  identifying 42
  in medicine 26, 42
  vinegar 23
Hyssop 8, 9, 10

  cultivation 13, 14, 17
  harvesting 18
  identifying 60
  in medicine 26
  propagation 15
  tea/tisane 17

I

infusions 24
inhalations 26
itches: treatments for 26

J

Jasmine: tea/tisane 20

L

Lady's mantle: in cosmetics 29
  cultivation 13, 17
  identifying 60
  in medicine 26
  tea/tisane 17
Lavender 6, 9, 10
  in cosmetics 27, 29
  cultivation 13, 14, 15
  harvesting 18
  identifying 60
  in medicine 26
  oil 23
  preserving 19
  propagation 15
  vinegar 23
Lemon balm 9, 62
  in cosmetics 29
  cultivation 14, 15, 17, 32
  harvesting 18
  identifying 32
  in medicine 26
  preserving 19
  propagation 15
  tea/tisane 20, 21
  vinegar 23
  see also Balm
Lemon thyme: cultivation 13
  vinegar 23
Lemon verbena: in cosmetics 29
  cultivation 15, 17
  harvesting 18
  identifying 60
  preserving 19
  tea/tisane 21
Lime: in cosmetics 27, 29
  harvesting 18
  identifying 60
  in medicine 26
  tea/tisane 21
Lovage 62
  in cosmetics 27, 29
  cultivation 13, 17, 43
  harvesting 18
  identifying 43
  in medicine 26, 43
  preserving 19
  tea/tisane 18

M

Madagascar periwinkle: in medicine 24
Marjoram 8, 10, 62
  in cosmetics 27
  cultivation 13, 14, 15, 16, 17
  harvesting 18
  identifying 44
  in medicine 26, 44
  oil 23
  preserving 19
  tea/tisane 18
  vinegar 23
  see also Pot marjoram, Sweet marjoram
Marigold: in cosmetics 27, 29
  cultivation 13, 14
  harvesting 18
  identifying 60
  in medicine 26
  preserving 19
migraines: treatment for 26
Mint 8, 9, 10
  in cosmetics 29
  cultivation 13, 14, 15, 17, 47
  harvesting 18
  identifying 47
  in medicine 26, 47
  preserving 19
  propagation 15
  tea/tisane 18, 20, 21
  vinegar 23
moisturisers 29
mouth: treatments for 26

N

Nasturtium 62
  in cosmetics 27
  cultivation 14
  identifying 61
  in medicine 26
  preserving 19
  vinegar 23
nausea: treatments for 26
Nettle: in compost 14
  in cosmetics 27, 29
  identifying 61
  in medicine 26

O

oils 22–23, 26
ointments 26
Opium poppy: in medicine 24
Oregano: in cosmetics 29
  cultivation 13, 48
  identifying 48
  in medicine 26, 48
  preserving 19
  propagation 15

P

Parsley 8, 9, 11, 62
  in cosmetics 29
  cultivation 13, 15, 17, 49
  harvesting 18
  identifying 49
  in medicine 26, 49
  preserving 19
Pelargonium: cultivation 14, 16, 17
  identifying 60
  see also Geranium
Pennyroyal: cultivation 14
  identifying 47
  in medicine 26
Peppermint: in cosmetics 27, 29
  cultivation 17
  identifying 47
  in medicine 26
  preserving 19
  tea/tisane 17
Pot marjoram: identifying 44, 45
poultices 26

R

rashes: treatment for 26
Raspberry: tea/tisane 21
  vinegar 23
Rauwolfia 10
Rocket: cultivation 50
  identifying 50
  in medicine 26, 50
Rose (wild): in cosmetics 29
  cultivation 17
  harvesting 18
  identifying 61
  vinegar 23
Rose hips 62
  in cosmetics 29
  in medicine 26
  tea/tisane 21
Rosemary 6, 8, 9, 10, 11
  in cosmetics 27, 29
  cultivation 13, 15, 16, 51
  harvesting 18
  identifying 51
  in medicine 26, 51
  oil 23
  preserving 18, 19
  propagation 15
  vinegar 23
Rue 10
  in cosmetics 29
  cultivation 13, 14
  harvesting 18
  identifying 61
  in medicine 26

S

Sage 6, 8, 9, 11
  in cosmetics 27, 29
  cultivation 13, 14, 15, 17, 52
  harvesting 18
  identifying 52
  in medicine 26, 52
  oil 23
  preserving 19
  propagation 15
  tea/tisane 18, 20
Salad burnet: in cosmetics 27, 29
  cultivation 15, 17, 53
  identifying 53
  in medicine 26, 53
  preserving 19
  propagation 15
  vinegar 23
"saunas", facial 27
Savory 6, 10, 62
  in cosmetics 29
  in medicine 26
  oil 23
  tea/tisane 18
  vinegar 23
  see also Summer savory, Winter savory
skin, improving 27
skin tonics/fresheners 29
slimming: treatments for 26
sore throat: treatments for 26
Sorrel 8
  identifying 61
  in medicine 26
  preserving 19
  propagation 15
Spearmint: identifying 47
spots: tonic for 29
stings: treatments for 26
Summer savory: cultivation 15, 17, 54
  harvesting 18
  identifying 54
  in medicine 54
  see also Savory, Winter savory
sunburn: treatment for 26
Sweet cicely 62
  cultivation 55
  harvesting 18
  identifying 55
  in medicine 26, 55
  preserving 19
  propagation 15
Sweet marjoram: cultivation 44
  identifying 44
Sweet woodruff: cultivation 13, 56
  identifying 56
  in medicine 56

T

Tansy: cultivation 14
  harvesting 18
  identifying 61
  propagation 15
Tarragon: cultivation 14, 15, 17, 57
  harvesting 18
  identifying 57
  in medicine 57
  oil 22
preserving 19
propagation 15
vinegar 23
teas/tisanes 21–21, 26
teeth: treatments for 26
Thyme 8, 9, 10, 11, 62
  in cosmetics 27
  cultivation 13, 14, 15, 17, 58
  harvesting 18
  identifying 58
  in medicine 26, 58
  oil 23
  preserving 19
  propagation 15
  vinegar 23
  see also Lemon thyme
treatments: antibiotic 26
  antiseptic 26, 27
  cleansing 26, 27
  disinfectant 26
  refreshing/tonic 26, 27, 29
  relaxing/sleep-inducing 26, 27

V

Valerian: in cosmetics 27
  harvesting 18
  identifying 61
  in medicines 26
veins/capillaries, broken: tonic for 29
Verbena: in cosmetics 29
  cultivation 16
  in medicines 26
  see also Lemon verbena
vinegars 23
Violet: in cosmetics 29
  identifying 61
  in medicines 26
  vinegar 23

W

Water mint: identifying 47
Watercress 62
White willow 9
Winter savory: cultivation 17
  propagation 15
Woodruff: cultivation 15, 17
  harvesting 18
  in medicine 26
  preserving 19
  propagation 15
  tea/tisane 20
  see also Sweet woodruff
wounds: treatments for 26
wrinkles: tonic for 29

Y

Yarrow: in compost 14
  in cosmetics 27, 29
  cultivation 17
  identifying 61
  in medicine 26
  tea/tisane 21

RECIPE INDEX

Bouquet garni 63

DESSERTS AND BAKING
Elderflower pancakes 107
Garlic herb French bread 107
Herb rye crispbread 107
Marigold pudding 106
Rosehip soup 106
Savoury country loaf 107
Stewed fruit with sweet cicely **106**

DRESSINGS
Basic herb vinaigrette dressing 65
Cold herb butters 65
Mayonnaise 65

DRINKS AND PRESERVES
Candied angelica 109
Candied flowers and leaves 109
Elderflower water 108
Herb jellies 109
Mint julep 108
Pickled nasturtium seeds 109
Red wine cup 108
Rose hip syrup 109
Woodruff cup 108

EGGS AND PASTA
Buttered eggs with herbs 92
Omelette aux fines herbs 93
Pizza Napoletana 92
Ravioli with ricotta 93
Spaghetti with pesto 93
Fines herbes 63

FISH AND SHELLFISH
Crab and mushroom mousse 80
Fish terrine with smoked eel and herbs 80
Herb baked trout 80
Kimbridge baked trout 77
Monkfish and spinach terrine with tomato and basil sauce 78
Poached salmon with dill sauce 76
Salmon mousse 79
Sea bass with herbs flambé 77
Sea bass with saffron, tomato and parsley mousse 78
Trout with lemon tarragon cream sauce 77
Salmon mousse 79
Sea bass with herbs flambé 77
Sea bass with saffron, tomato and parsley mousse 78
Trout with lemon tarragon cream sauce 77

MEAT
Beef fillet in puff pastry with mustard and chervil sauce 90
Gammon with parsley and mushroom sauce 87

Green pork and green dumplings 88
Lamb korma 91
Lamb medallions with tarragon 88
Lemon and herb fillet steaks 86
Marinated pork chops 88
Meat loaf 87
Pork fillet Wellington 87
Roast belly of pork with rosemary potatoes 90
Saltimbocca 87
Steamed best end of lamb with rosemary 91

POULTRY AND GAME
Chicken and thyme pie 82
Chicken Kiev 83
Chicken lemon sauté 82
Guinea fowl with scallions and sweet herbs 85
Lemon and herb baked chicken 83
Raised game pie 85
Roast chicken 84
Sautéed chicken with wine and mushrooms 83
Steamed chicken and avocado with tarragon and vermouth sauce 82

SAUCES
Béarnaise sauce 64
Béchamel sauce 64
Green sauce 65
Herb butter sauces 65
Horseradish sauce 64
Mint sauce 64
Sorrel sauce 65
Tarragon, dill or fennel sauce 65

SOUPS
Bean soup 66
Cream of winter soup 69
Garlic soup 66
Iced cucumber and mint soup 69
Lettuce and mint soup 69
Lovage soup 67
Mussel soup with thyme 67
Nettle soup 69
Rose hip soup 106
Summer soup 67
Tomato and rosemary soup 66

STARTERS (see also Soups)
Bouillabaisse 73
Butter beans hors d'oeuvre 73
Ceviche 74
Chervil quiche 74
Creamy sage and onion flan 75
Game pâté 70
Gâteau of green vegetables 72
Herby cheese dip with crudités 71
Nut pâté 70
Pakoras with mint chutney 75

Pâté with spinach and herbs 70
Potted ham with rosemary 69
Shrimp-filled avocados 70
Sorrel and red onion tart 75
Tomato and mint water ice 75
Water souchet 72

STOCKS
Bone stock 63
Brown stock 63
Chicken or game bird stock 64
Court bouillon 64
Fish stock 64
Vegetable stock 63
White stock 63

VEGETABLE AND SALADS
Avocado and orange mint salad 102
Carrot casserole 96
Cauliflower with sorrel sauce 97
Chick-peas à la Grecque 103
Cucumber raita salad 95
Dandelion greens with bacon 99
Eggplant à la Nîmoise 98
English potato and parsley patties 94

Fattoush 104
Fennel braised with apple 102
French peas 103
Glorious salad, a 100
Green beans with Tarragon 104
Herb baked new potatoes 100
Lemon and herb cauliflower 99
Lima beans with savory 96
Millet croquettes 94
Mushrom and herb casserole 96
Mushrooms poached with lemon and herbs 102
Peas with grapefruit and mint 97
Persian rice with herbs 98
Pole beans with garlic and sage 102
Potato raita 95
Potato salad 94
Potato sticks 95
Potatoes braised in red wine 100
Stuffed cucumber 95
Stuffed peppers 100
Tabbouli 98
Turnips braised with bacon and sage 97
Zucchini with lemon and herbs 104

CREDITS – RECIPES

BRITISH MEAT: 86, 88, 91; BRITISH TROUT ASSOCIATION: 65, 74, 77, 80; SUSAN FLEMING: 63, 67, 74, 87, 96, 106, 108, 109; MUSHROOM GROWERS ASSOCIATION: 80, 87, 103; NATIONAL DAIRY COUNCIL: 69, 71, 75, 87, 91, 102.

Recipes on pp. 67, 72, 88, 100, 106 derived from Elisabeth Ayrton's **English Provincial Cooking** (Mitchell Beazley, 1980); Recipes on pp. 95, 107, 109 derived from Colin Tudge's **Future Cook** (Mitchell Beazley, 1980). Identifying Herbs extracts 31–61 derived from the herb section of **The Cook Book** by Terence & Caroline Conran (Mitchell Beazley 1980)

CREDITS – ILLUSTRATIONS

Bay Picture Library: 79T, 95TR, 96–97B, 98–99, 104–5; The Bodleian Library: 8BL; British Meat: 88CB, 89, 90T; Linda Burgess: 18TL, 18–19T; The Mansell Collection: 9TL, 10BL, 10TR, 11CT, 11TL; Milk Marketing Board: 70–71, 74B, 86BL, 91BL; Mushroom Growers Association: 81, 87TR; National Dairy Council: 68; Uitgeverij het Spectrum B.V. 1974: 24–25; Hans Verkroost: 1, 6, 12–14 (all pictures), 16TR; Zefa: 28; MB: Bryce Attwell: 102–103B; Roger Philips: 30, 72–73; Clive Streeter: 78T.

T = Top, B = Bottom, TL = Top Left, TR = Top Right, C = Centre